EMBRACING MY

DARKNESS AND LIGHT

AT THE SAME TIME.

THE STUDENT

REFLECTIONS OF THE HEART AND MIND

ÖZLEM ÖZKAN

FOR MY ANCESTORS AND LIFELONG
TEACHERS.

When there was no sound.
I held my pen.
When there was no voice.
I wrote.
Heart to heart.
Soul to soul.

— ÖÖ

CONTENTS

A NOTE TO THE READER

"Knowing others is intelligence; knowing yourself is true wisdom. Mastering others is strength; mastering yourself is true power," said Lao Tzu. Although I cannot claim to have achieved self mastery, I believe that through continuous practice of self examination, the process of writing this book and not forgetting a life experience of more than three decades allowed me to know crucial parts of myself. It took courage and determination to get to know myself, to face my light and darkness and at the same time acknowledge that my own strength lies in my own vulnerability and authenticity.

The Student is the story of my continuous journey of being a student of life and getting to know myself. It took time, but I finally first identified parts of myself and second, analyzed how these parts affected my entire life as well as those around me. I lived in three different countries, Denmark, the Netherlands and Turkey, and traveled across four continents where I interacted with a variety of people. Those people have held a place for me, with an act of immense open heartedness, to express and reflect on the deepest truth of who I am. While this book reflects on my own life, I believe it has value for everyone. You can safely read my experiences from your own comfortable setting, and perhaps you might relate to those experiences. Even more, this book engages your heart and not just your mind, it speaks to your whole being.

The Student includes true stories and to protect the privacy of those concerned, all names have been changed. The true stories are short and all have a common theme of "getting to know yourself." It can be read chronologically or you can open a random page and start with a story.

Taken at the right place and time with confidence and integrity, this book might make you recognize yourself in some of the writings. I suggest you read it slowly one story at a time. Allow yourself to pause for a moment and reflect. You can re-read the same stories many times, and every time you might have a new insight.

I am eager to share what I have learned and that's why I have put an intensified attention and energy into writing this book. While it wasn't easy (re)visiting some of my darkness, I have written this book with an open heart and enjoyed the journey. I hope that you will also enjoy and reap the benefits these stories may have to offer. I wish for this book to serve as an inspiration for your own life and for you to start to get to know yourself, right here, right now.

— Özlem Özkan
Amsterdam, the Netherlands

INTRODUCTION

Shine so much that you and others believe in light.
Light up your tongue, hand, eyes, actions.
Light is infinite.
Every action will be surrounded by sparks of light.
And know that.
Light comes with darkness.
For the believers of light believe also in darkness.
Have the courage.
Go to and through the darkness.
The light will be the brightest ever.

— ÖÖ

Playlist for The Student

Like every single baby, when being in the womb of her mother, I believe that I was trusting the whole process. I was trusting that my heart would beat, all my organs would be created, my limbs would arise, my brain, nose, eyes, mouth, and ears would all arise. Laying down in the womb of my mother, there shouldn't be a worry about the future or thinking of the past or asking yourself why you were going to come on Earth. I just was. My mother was proudly waiting for her own baby to come, dreaming about me and surrounded by love in a rose garden. After birth, being the caterpillar, leaning on my mother's breast, knowing that the energy in her aura was clear as the sky and full as the air in the forest, the light around her was bright as the sun and the ground she was on was Mother Earth that firmly held her and me. She knew that I would start as a caterpillar and find my way in a place where I was no longer the caterpillar but not yet a butterfly.

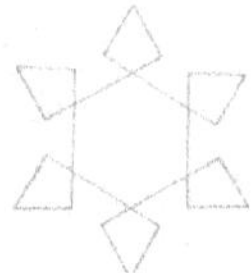

I was born to Turkish parents in the Netherlands. Before my parents came to the Netherlands they were farmers in a small village in Turkey. Although science was slightly involved in their life, especially in the agriculture part, most of the time their actions were based either on intuition or fear. After arriving in the Netherlands, being a foreigner in an unfamiliar land, their thinking about labor shifted from farming to education. Having lost their hope about their own education, they wanted to make sure their three children studied. My parents were ready to spend their last penny on everything that aligned with this big mission.

On one hand, by believing that my life was easier than what my parents went through, I felt that I had to make sure I made a difference in the world. My parents and I believed that road went through education. If my parents put all of their cards of life on the table to make their children study, then I had to make sure I did and created a difference in the world. I felt motivated because I enjoyed learning, but at the same time I felt a huge pressure on my being. Whatever it would cost, even my life, I was born into this world to get every single thing out of me, strive until I made a difference, not only in our family but also in the world. This feeling and the enormous pressure I put on my small shoulders made me feel anxious, but I kept going and I didn't plan to stop. While I was studying full time and gained a Master degree, I was working since my teenage years in part-time positions in commercial sales while completing my studies.

Yet, I remember as a child wanting to be like a butterfly. I freely wanted to inhale the air that I felt like breathing and exhale at a place where I wanted to be. And I believed my wings were very big to make me fly to far lands, wander, and meet people. I believed my heart was able to expand so much that I could inhale anything, even the unfamiliar. I believed the unfamiliar land for my parents, the Netherlands, became my familiar and I was a wanderer of the unfamiliar to make eventually my familiar. Why was the unfamiliar intimidating and at the same time very attractive to me?

But who was I really? Was I the one who was only focused on studying and "making a difference" in the world or was I the little child, the wanderer and imaginer? And how could I know who I really was?

I found myself in a place between giving up and fighting, exactly in the middle of this feeling, being between light and darkness, being between the eve of losing and starting a new life. If I'd stay it would hurt and if I'd go it would cost my life...

I have never been the girl that liked the typical "girly" things such as playing with makeup and collecting dolls. My mother told me that she used to like playing with dolls as a child, but I didn't. She even got dolls for her wedding chest. When she was a teenager she knitted long dresses for these dolls. These dolls were presented in our glass cabinet in the living room and literally no one was allowed to touch it, except for me. My mother even encouraged me to play with them sometimes. Although I liked how they looked, I wasn't into dolls. I was never interested in makeup either. I believed makeup was only going to ruin my face and why should I put something on that would make me ugly?

What I loved was being on the streets. The street was my zone where I received and sought comfort. It became my biggest love. My childhood was centered around going to school until the late afternoon and then playing outside until dark. When the school bell rang in the late afternoon, I ran home to save every single minute for my play time. I was this girl whose mother made her eat and drink something right after school, and I did it fast so I could run outside to play. My mother was rigorous in cleaning and made sure to dress me with clean clothes. But I was and would keep disappointing her, because coming back from outside I tracked some dirt into our home. Although I cared a little bit to keep my clothes and body clean so I could get approval from my mother, what I really cared about was play, with or without dirt, it didn't matter.

My parents tried to get us whatever equipment we needed to play outside. Since they were tight with money they balanced purchases between new items and second-hand items, and I often found raw equipment on the street. Every single thing on the street was my equipment to play and create play. While playing, the trees became bases to stop when playing softball. The benches became the gate to score a goal playing soccer. The pieces of an old bed that we found in the trash became our trampoline. The old orange roof-top stones became chalk to draw hopscotch. The forest was meant for camping with all the old clothes we got from my parents and sticks found in the streets. Dodgeball was mostly played against a garage with a second-hand ball from the thrift market. Little holes around the trees were used as marble holes and it was always easy to go marble hunting to find ones in the bushes. One day my mother said she couldn't get new rubber bands or elastics for me to play with, so I closed a deal with a postman who brought mail every day with short elastics. After getting many elastics in just a few days from this postman, I cut them and knotted them together to have a long elastic in order to play the elastic game. I always felt I had so much because on the street I could create anything at any given moment. On weekends, even at lunch, I preferred to eat outside on the grass behind our apartment building where we pulled daisies afterward to create necklaces and hair bands. The streets were my oyster, a refuge of everything and many moments of being one in and with the flow.

Although I never attended a sport club where they taught how to play sports, I taught myself to play different sports because I loved it. Playing tennis and badminton was a major outside activity for me. With a tennis ball, I made sure it touched all grounds in my neighborhood. I only had two tennis rackets, a tennis ball, and badminton shuttle, so I used the racket for tennis and badminton. I often played badminton with my brother or friends and played many imaginary games with the racket. We had a large wall in our neighborhood. Sometimes if I didn't have anyone to play tennis with, I brought my racket and tennis ball there and practiced playing tennis for hours and hours. I still joke with my father and tell him, "If you had sent me to a tennis club, I would have played with Serena Williams or Martina Hingis." It was actually not a joke back then, because with my child courage I believed it.

When I was playing anything such as tag, dodgeball, tennis, badminton, elastics or a self-taught game my mind was clear and free from confusions. I forgot every single thing and was only present with play. I became one with the deep presence of life.

On one hand my parents loved my play and hustle mentality, but on the other hand I sometimes got comments not only from my parents but also from my surroundings about how I wasn't playing like a girl and wasn't keeping myself clean. My face was mostly dirty because of balls hit at my face while playing. My hands and nails were black because of all the dust and soil from playing marbles. The colors of my clothes faded away because they touched most of the stones on the street. I got holes in my t-shirts and jackets because I ran through trees and bushes to not be caught while playing tag. My hair was always kept short, not only to keep the house clean, but it was easy and safe when playing outside. So, nothing was really typical for a girl in the sense of the "typical girl" my parents, school and society had constructed.

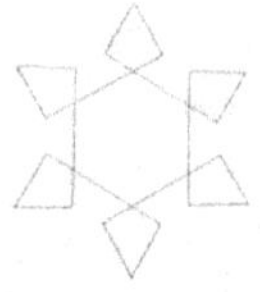

Primary school was a breeze for me. I easily received good scores without much effort and I was fast, magnificently fast. I loved the reading tests at school where the teacher was measuring the pace I was reading. There was a list of words and you had to read them one by one as fast as you could. I remember sometimes I forgot to breathe while reading the words because I was fast and the only thing I wanted to do was be fast, get faster, be the fastest, the best. I picked things up very quickly. While this helped me I also felt that I was standing out from the crowd. I often started questioning the status quo. It helped and allowed me to discover the undiscovered. This path was often a path of loneliness. Despite having many people around me, feeling a real connection to them was difficult. The idea I had about myself was that I was different, sometimes better, sometimes worse, but almost never similar or equal. Even though I kept telling myself that I was born to stand out, deep down I didn't like it. I really wanted to have deep connections to people, but I found it difficult.

Being competitive was in me, since the first day of school and the first moment I started playing with my brother or friends, I always wanted to win. My winning attitude was a huge part of me, especially winning from others. When someone else was involved, I wanted to win from that person no matter what. Sometimes I was scared that I'd hurt myself because of my extreme hunger for winning. Think about a leopard, for instance, trying to catch its prey. He would do anything and everything he could to catch his prey. When I was studying or playing I wanted to give all of myself, everything or nothing, and there was nothing in between. After I went back home from competing, I was left with two feelings. One was that I was super happy with "winning" the game and automatically I appreciated myself and felt appreciated by those in my surroundings. The other feeling was a much darker feeling— guilt. A dark feeling, felt intensely in my body which brought me from time-to-time a lack of sleep and nightmares. I was aware that my winning and giving everything mentality often harmed other people which made me feel guilty.

I wanted to compete with high-flyers at school and during play I preferred playing with boys since I believed back then that they were more competitive, and I wanted to take that battle. I played and yelled so hard when winning and I was aware the other person felt hurt or maybe even felt like a loser. I could feel that I wasn't really lifting up others with my winning mentality, I was bringing them down and at the same time I believed I wasn't supposed to do that. Even though my winning mentality served many teammates and places I belonged to, the dark feeling in me kept existing. After striving for many years only to win from others, I saw that some people didn't like me anymore. To be truthful I didn't think about others, only myself. Yet again, the great feeling of winning and less great feeling of guilt went hand-in-hand together.

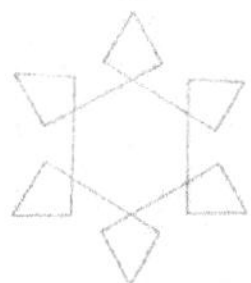

I experienced my journey from a caterpillar to butterfly as a continuous process, I was no longer a caterpillar but not yet a butterfly. And in this journey, I observed, learned, failed, evolved, realized and loved. I knew that I was a seeker. The search for knowledge about the universe and myself and the continuous longing for love created a journey which was accompanied by many journeys to different lands, people and cultures. And in this journey, I knew that I wanted to listen to my soul, what whispers within me, and create my own journey, guided by my bigger source, entwined in faith. This journey was going to be nothing but a journey from within—even if this meant from time-to-time loneliness, confusion, and not feeling understood.

My journey within wasn't a romantic one, which I previously believed it should be. It isn't a story with only good catchy experiences and happy endings. Yet, it was a journey of different feelings at the same time: despair, happiness, fear, and joy. In this journey I came to realize that joy can be in anything I experience, and I still strive to experience joy in everything around me.

In this journey I reflect on my light and darkness which often walked hand-in-hand. It taught me to accept, surrender, find a reward in my light as well as in my darkness, and allow life to calmly reveal its own secret.

1. FEAR

Christian, Jew, Muslim, shaman, Zoroastrian, stone, ground, mountain, river, each has a secret way of being with the mystery, unique and not to be judged.

— Jalal ad-Din Muhammad Rumi

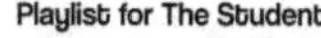

Playlist for The Student

My parents taught me the values they grew up with in their village in the Aegean region of Turkey. Being Turkish and Muslim were important to them, especially because we lived in a country initially foreign to my parents and these identities were not dominant identities in the Netherlands. Often, I used to affirm two words: *Türküm* and *Müslümanım* for my parents which were the same affirmations that they had grown up with. Although these words are only two words in Turkish, when you translate them into Dutch or English they become sentences. The first one, *Türküm,* means "I am a Turk" and the second word means "I am a Muslim." My parents, my father when he was fourteen and my mother when she was twenty, had all of a sudden stepped into a completely new culture. But it wasn't only a new culture, they changed from living in a primitive village in Turkey to living in a modern city in Europe, leaving their village where people lived their life by Muslim values to a more liberal society where most people are atheists and where you could find marks of Calvinism. I experienced my parents being persistent in wanting to keep their core identity around being a Turk and Muslim. The two words *Türküm* and *Müslümanım,* which I was never to forget, were given to me on my small shoulders. It was beautiful and pretty confusing at the same time. Beautiful because I felt a strong attachment and belonging to the culture and religion and it was a space where I could express my authentic self. But, on the other hand, I often did not know how to handle the confusion I was experiencing when going through daily life, blending Dutch and Turkish culture, and trying to adhere to the two words created more confusion in me.

I wasn't sure if it was the way my parents brought this up or my rebellious part, but I didn't like that I *had to* state the two Turkish words. I often said them to please my parents even though I sometimes didn't feel like it. Sometimes I was rebellious and would tell my parents that I didn't want to say them. But at the same time, I was afraid my parents would disapprove of me and they would think I wasn't being a Turk or Muslim. There was a fear of becoming disassociated from these words, these values. I definitely felt a certain way of being Turkish and also Muslim. I felt attached to my roots, yet from a young age, I liked the idea of exploring other nationalities and religions too. Could these coexist?

I believed that for my family, being a Turk and Muslim were very important because that was something familiar to them. They were very protective of their identity and I believed they were even scared to lose that identity. They were holding onto it like a child walking on a balancing bench. The tighter they kept holding onto it, the less trust there was, the easier it was to fall down. What if they just trusted the process, what would have happened then? My parents accepted and respected other nationalities and religions but the unfamiliarity and unknown made them very protective of me exploring something or someone "foreign." As a rebel, I did it anyway because from a young age I believed I thought differently, not better or worse, just differently. I believed my family was fearful of the unknown and at the same time biased by all things they were hearing from their environment, especially the media, and family back in Turkey. Although I didn't fully agree with them, there was a seed of fear planted somewhere in my mind: "Be mindful of foreign people, religions and things."

2011 - *Istanbul, Turkey*

Here I was, having grown up in the Netherlands with the two words in Turkish, *Türküm* and *Müslümanım,* and now I found myself living in Turkey itself. I was only twenty-four and I was living and teaching in Istanbul. Affirmations of *Türküm* and *Müslümanım* had been out of my life for years. But in a very specific situation, which came unexpectedly, I was forced to revisit these words.

I worked at an international school and had a student with the most beautiful eyes and heart. Her name was Rojin and she was Kurdish—an ethnicity which I had heard a lot about when I was growing up in the 90's and an ethnicity of which I was supposed to keep a distance from most of the time. For example, in the 90's in the Netherlands with Turkish television, I often heard news about conflicts in Turkey between Turkish and Kurdish people. I never knew what was really going on but I remember the images and stories of people being killed or kidnapped, which created in me a suspicion and distrust towards Kurdish people. Having a close

Kurdish friend in high school made me partly explore my beliefs about Kurdish people but I was still firm to keep a distance. But a few years later, after receiving a text message concerning an event that had happened involving the death of this Kurdish high school friend, I made a rigid decision to create a firm distance to anyone with a Kurdish background. She had been killed by her husband, who was also of Kurdish ethnicity. I was consumed by emotions of grief, anger and fear. I remember struggling to understand how this could have happened. The idea of someone killing another human being had never touched my life so vividly and forcefully before. I never learned the full details of this murder, and I wasn't aware this cruel incident could happen to anyone from any ethnicity, but I made the connection to being Kurdish. In consequence, I made the conclusion that I had to be careful of Kurdish people as my fear directed me.

However, I had a student in my class and I had to teach her, maybe also teach myself during this period. While my heart wanted to meet her at a place where she was a person regardless of her ethnicity, my mind was fearful. Rojin was such a bright student. Her caring heart was quickly recognized by me and other students. She was a very skinny, big-eyed girl and very helpful. Rojin almost never needed explanations a second time because she picked up instructions very easily and even had time left to explain to other students. From time-to-time Rojin was shy, but the more we connected the more she started being courageous and started asking more insightful questions, questions I never dreamed about. She was extremely respectful towards others, not only towards me and other teachers, but to any single person at school, from students in my class to cleaners, from the reception people to the facility staff. I wasn't fully sure if she always agreed with the things I said, but I could feel strongly that her upbringing at home made sure that respect was one of the virtues in her life so she did her outermost best to respect other people. Rojin was evolving so well, but I still had a way to go. Things were very complex in my mind. The two words I grew up with *Türküm* and *Müslümanım*, the media in the 90's, my Kurdish high school friend who was killed years ago, were all fighting with the fact that this Kurdish girl was one of the most respectful and helpful people I had ever met. She was nothing I thought I knew, only kind and loving. There was an immense conflict and at the same time a gap between my limiting beliefs about Kurdish ethnicity and my new experience with this Kurdish student.

As kind as Rojin was, her mother was a very empathetic, compassionate and grateful woman. As an act of thanking me for teaching her daughter, she persistently invited me to their house for tea time. While I didn't want to offend her by turning down her offer, I was very nervous, afraid and ambivalent at the same time. I thought I was an open-minded person, well-traveled, had enough different friends from various cultures, nationalities, and backgrounds. Yet, why did I feel fear when I received Rojin's mother's invitation? I was anxious, scared that these lovely people would do something to me, maybe manipulate me, or might start saying bad things about Turks. My fear for Kurdish people was so deeply planted that I could not shrug it off or forget it. But I knew that keeping my distance from Kurdish people and staying in my comfort zone wouldn't push me beyond my own judgments already made about them from my past. If I truly wanted to have a different and better experience than the mental repeat in my head I first had to believe that I could have a new experience.

After a few sleepless nights, mental preparation, and really deciding to want to overcome my fear and get rid of my judgements, I went to Rojin's house. When I entered the house, there was an old lady, Rojin's grandmother, sitting on the couch with one leg crossed under her and the other leg resting on the couch. She wore a traditional hand-made crochet lace headscarf and her hands, covered with henna, were holding prayer beads. Her head was slightly bent and watching her prayer beads, it was all accompanied by little gratitude and oneness prayers that she stated with a soft voice. When she saw me, she slowly put her head up and gazed at me with a smile. With a calming voice she said, "Welcome my child, may you bring honor to our house." I could feel the goosebumps spread over my body. I walked over and kissed her hand and put it on my forehead. Hand-kissing was something I had been taught to do since a young age, and my parents wanted to keep this Turkish tradition to greet and show respect to elders in our daily life. Rojin's grandmother's loving presence was extremely felt and warmly welcomed. I started questioning myself, how could these lovely people do something to me? I had to change the way I thought. It wasn't true that I had to be fearful of the Kurdish ethnicity. The only truth was this family's love and kindness. In their house I felt that I was treated as their own daughter and they made more than sure that I was comfortable. After teatime I was even invited to their restaurant to have dinner with them. I remember the welcoming staff when we entered the restaurant and them vocalizing the thought if I was Kurdish because of my looks. After we ordered dinner, I heard this sentence, *"Başım gözüm üstüne."* This sentence means, "I accept your request with respect and would do my outermost best to fulfill it." They also left a present for me in the form of a phrase, *choni bashi?*, meaning "how are you" in Kurdish. This sentence nowadays allows me to connect to any Kurdish person I meet on Earth, and on top of that, it is fueled with curiosity to that person and reminds me of Rojin's family and their warm heart. Above all, it reminds me to cut my own judgments to ribbons.

2. DISTRUST

Come, let us all be friends for once.
Let us make life easy on us.
Let us be lovers and loved ones.
The earth shall be left to no one.

— Yunus Emre

2014 - In the air, between Tokyo, Japan and Beijing, China.

When flying from Tokyo to Beijing we had to make an emergency landing due to bad weather conditions. I found myself at a small Chinese airport, yet, I am not even sure if it was an airport. It was very dark outside and I couldn't really see much out of the tiny airplane window beyond the tarmac and since I started panicking I didn't listen clearly to the initial announcement by the flight attendant. Once we had landed, most people stood up and in the excitement and commotion of the sudden change in destination, they all started talking at once and looking at each other with questioning faces and tense body postures. Most were Asian and even though I was comfortable around different cultures and languages and able to pick up words in several languages, I was so confused and didn't understand anything people were saying. I only had my senses to work with and in the heightening confusion and commotion I tried to understand people's body language and facial expressions, but the only thing I accomplished was becoming panicked and anxious as well. Due to my fear and distrust of the unknown I drove myself into a state of anxiety and nervousness while we were asked to remain seated on the plane. Unable to remain calm, I started to hyperventilate and sweat profusely. The thought that we would all die and the smell of Asian food contributed to my panic feeling that I was in a movie scene of sorts, not really knowing what was going on—panicked people, a new announcement that we had to stay in the airplane until the next announcement—I only wanted this movie scene to be over and the next scene for me to be chilling in my bed with a movie on and if possible with a loved one next to me. I only wanted to feel safe, and now I was feeling many things but safe.

My specific seat on the plane was on the far left side of a row of four seats next to the aisle in the middle part of the plane. I had thought the middle section of the plane was a great spot to view what was happening in front and behind at any given time. But in this situation, the behavior and emotions of so many confused, anxious, and afraid people overwhelmed me. Through the loud talking I noticed a Western-looking man a row behind. All of a sudden, I felt a calmness wash through me, edging out the panicked, anxious, and confused fibers from my body. Since I felt extremely unsafe and panicked, I was sort of screaming to feel safe. Assuming the man understood and spoke English, I started speaking English to him and asked him what was happening. He knew as little as I knew, we had to make an emergency landing due to bad weather conditions. I asked the man where he was from because since a young age, I used to ask where someone was from in order to label and at the same time clarify and decide based on the person's answer if I was safe or unsafe. To my surprise, this man was from the Netherlands and was living with his family in Beijing, working for a Dutch organization. I felt one more time a calmness wash through my body, a calmness that you have when you enter a warm bath with your favorite soothing music on in the background. A calmness when you taste your favorite food again after a long time of fasting. A calmness like when a close friend tells you that everything is alright. I was in awe. Someone was there from the same country as where I was born and raised, nothing to feel unsafe about I told myself.

We started talking about life, living and working as a foreigner abroad. I really liked talking about these topics because growing up with two totally different cultures, Dutch and Turkish, made me question each time again who I was and where I was from. Even though I knew I had parents from Turkey and was raised in the Netherlands, I believed that my ancestors might have been from other countries. Talking to this newly met man in the plane started as small talk but ended being a talk for hours. It took around six hours before the plane started taking off for Beijing. In the meantime, there wasn't much of my panic left, because I had directed my attention to talking to this man in the present moment. I was still a little bit insecure and felt awkward, but I definitely wanted to hide this from the man. I didn't want him to know how I felt, instead I sketched an image for him about a courageous girl who traveled the world alone. I thought that showing my true emotions to someone would make me weak so I pretended something else to appear strong. Hiding my insecurity and fear, I kept talking to this man. He was kind, a good listener, a great questioner. In only six hours, we connected on a level of the heart and there was lots of laughter. I still don't know if this man recognized my fear and insecurity, but I do know he was a kind man and made me feel comfortable. There was something in this man's energy, something undefined, a goodness that was protecting me from my own fear.

Arriving at Beijing at two o'clock in the morning instead of eight the night before resulted in losing the hotel shuttle pick up from the airport. I didn't have an international phone to call my hotel and I had limited prepaid minutes on my phone. Being exhausted, I wanted to go to the hotel to sleep a few hours before going back to the airport in the early morning to catch my flight to Istanbul and the next flight on to Washington, D.C. The kind man that I talked to in the plane offered to take me to my hotel. Outside in the dark standing next to this man, I felt scared. First of all, I was scared of the dark and not seeing taxis and many people around. Secondly, I briefly had some scary movie scenes playing through my mind of the more negative, scary situations if I were to accept his offer. For a moment, I was again caught by first my own judgements and then my fear. This time I decided to not lead myself by fear but by heart. Going back to my heart, I knew that he was a kind and good man—he only wanted to help. I started to surrender to the situation and trust my intuition. So, I trusted this unknown man and accepted his offer and took the ride. On a very dark night where I could just make out the stars, where there weren't many light posts outside, I ended up making it safely to my end-destination and all the nervousness and anxiety had left my body by then. My heart brought me to the right place, there wasn't anything to fear. The man dropped me, thanked me, and left to go to his family.

3. BIAS

Sometimes it's hard
To accept
You don't know.
To accept
You only think that you know.
Sometimes it takes only
To surrender to all of that is
To the known and unknown.
It takes courage
To surrender to all that is.
It takes courage
To shed off your beliefs
And meet a person
In a sacred place
Where he is a person.
It comes with a gift
Opening hearts
To ways never imagined and never known
Fueled with love.

— ÖÖ

Playlist for The Student

Event X - Istanbul, Turkey - 24-year-old self.

Why did you decide to become a teacher? How do you connect your lessons to the real world? Why do you want to teach at this school? How would you handle a difficult situation? First, at the age of twenty-four, I compulsively researched all possible questions I could get when interviewing for a teaching position at an international school in Istanbul. Second, I compulsively memorized all possible questions and answers in English that might make me become hired for the teaching job. I went to the interview and was able to convince the owner of my English ability from the sentences I had memorized, resulting in securing the position. One year later my level of English tremendously increased, and I was interviewing for another international school in Istanbul. This time, I chose to be real about my English skills. By wanting to be authentic and at the same time a perfectionist about my English, I told the owner that I was sometimes insecure about English and after admitting that, I got an intense release. This had been one critical thing I hadn't been brave enough to tell openly and actually chose to hide. When the school owner asked me if I spoke Turkish, since he knew that I was born and raised by Turkish parents in the Netherlands, I said that I spoke a little bit, but not good enough. Although this answer was true or false depending on how you look at it, I certainly believed that I was lying because I was afraid to be judged on the way I spoke Turkish by Turkish coworkers and some parents with Turkish backgrounds. I spoke Turkish, yet I believed that my Turkish wasn't the so-called "Istanbul Turkish." I was ashamed of the Turkish accent I had learned from my parents which they had acquired while growing up in their village in Turkey. I wasn't confident but embarrassed to own it and talk Turkish the way I did. I believed that being recognized as a great teacher with great ideas, hard work, good work, important connections and forward motions were all dependent on great accents.

Event Y - South-Netherlands - 13-year-old self.

When I was in secondary school at the age of thirteen, my parents wanted to send me to a boarding school which focused on regular Dutch education and religious education. When I toured this boarding school in the south of the Netherlands, they took us to a large room where they told us that students from the boarding school became teachers of the boarding school, that teaching was a virtue of itself and is sacred. After the tour my parents didn't identify with the values of this school and decided to not send me, however, they indirectly gave me something that stayed with me forever, the experience of this large room. In my last year of high school, I decided I wanted to be a part of this virtue called "teaching." I wanted to teach, challenge mindsets, and teach goodness. I had received a good education among the formal (Bachelor and Master in Education) and non formal educational settings around me which made me ready to then give back the knowledge and wisdom I had accumulated. Like Maya Angelou stated, "When you get, give; when you learn, teach."

While the person in Event X seemed like someone with low moral standards and high ambition who would do anything to get what she wanted, the person in Event Y seemed like someone who wanted to uphold the teaching profession with integrity and high ideals. But in fact, I went through both events. As our days bounce between darkness and light, I often bounced between being someone who tried to reach her goal by any means necessary and someone who upheld the teacher profession with integrity.

2009 - Istanbul, Turkey

Being a classroom teacher at international schools in Istanbul was a blessing for the idealist me. At one international school I was privileged to teach students for three consecutive years. I was their classroom teacher in reception class, grade one and then in grade two. They came from faraway lands and different cultures. In a class with more than fifteen nationalities, days were busy and tiring. I had students from Finland, Spain, Mexico, Bulgaria, Iran, England, the Netherlands, Libya, Turkey, Israel, Argentina, China, Saudi Arabia, Syria, Pakistan, and Canada. While the main language was English at school, hearing different languages in the classroom and playground was normal. Flags of different countries hung on the walls and innocent-hearted students' faces representing the world population were trying, learning, creating and evolving. When things became difficult for them, they didn't give up, they kept trying. Even though those children came from different households, cultures, and religions, they had a common ground in this classroom. They were all students looking for a place where they could feel safe to learn and explore. Even children from two different countries where politicians could not even have a chat without arguing were more than friends. My students respected and protected each other, learned from each other and became connected with every single person in the classroom.

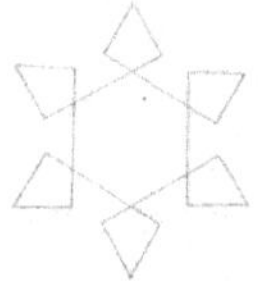

In Istanbul, some days I woke up tired and I had to keep motivating the ideal teacher in me. I told myself in bed the following sentence, *"Today, you have a chance to teach one child, change his life forever."* This sentence made me get out of bed and put me into the flow of the day. Being in the flow didn't always mean that things went smoothly. Teaching children meant being in an environment with a lot of noise. Due to my sensitivity to noise, I was sometimes dizzy which made it difficult for me to handle sometimes. I discovered that creating structure in the classroom would prevent unnecessary screams and ended up being good for me and for the students. When I had structure and rules in the classroom, the children knew what they could expect from me and I knew exactly what I could expect from them. Teaching math, reading, science, music, physical education and some other subjects as a classroom teacher was enjoyable. Yet, my favorite subject was social emotional education. I loved doing activities with children about their feelings. I believed that their feelings were connected to their performances in school and life. I believed if I contributed to the social and emotional awareness and intelligence of my students, they would have a great foundation for their life.

After a few years of teaching during the summer holiday, I got the news that I would get a British student in the classroom in the new academic year. His parents were living for some years in Istanbul and had four children, one of them was Ethan. When I heard that Ethan and his family were British, I started becoming nervous. I was even more nervous when I got to know that Ethan was a child with special needs, had a different way of learning and had additional selective attention for some topics. In my teaching career, I had just started being comfortable with teaching, especially teaching in English, yet even the thought of Ethan being a native speaker of English and his unique learning requirements triggered my insecurity and perfectionism. I didn't know how to handle the situation. I didn't trust I was capable enough to handle this. The two challenges that were waiting for me were teaching grade one English reading and writing in the international curriculum for the first time and teaching Ethan, who had a unique way of learning. While I was comfortable teaching reading and writing in Dutch and screening and testing children with special needs, teaching reading and writing in English and teaching a child with special needs was from a different dimension.

The first day with Ethan at school resulted in a frustrated child and a very frustrated teacher. Ethan was definitely learning and thinking differently than most children, and more so than most children in grade one. In those first few weeks, Ethan tested me and explored how far he could go in challenging me. At school, I pretended to be confident but at home I prayed I could find enough strength to make it through those long days. However, I later realized I had already judged Ethan and put him in a box in my mind even before he started because of the stories and reports I had heard and read. I believed Ethan was sent to me, to challenge me in different ways and eventually make me evolve, but it didn't take my judgement and insecurity away. I knew I could only evolve if I started seeing Ethan as whole. By trying to learn more about him through him, day-by-day I started establishing a connection with Ethan. At the time, all the books and articles I had studied on developmental psychology, education, pathology, special needs and disorders just weren't making much sense to me. The real challenge was to meet someone without acknowledging any prior labels and instead allow the person to determine the path to take and which identities to cultivate. I had to know a person through the person, by connecting to him, accepting him, and trusting him and the process.

Ethan is one of my biggest teachers which led me to a path that I might not have ever discovered and walked if not for him. I made a plan, edited it sometimes and proposed it to Ethan and his mother. In this plan it was to first respect each other, then structure the learning environment and infuse it with mutual agreement. The first step of this plan was if Ethan wanted to say something, he only had to raise his hand. This part was actually very simple and from the simplicity came growth. By only raising his hand, Ethan started showing respect to everyone in the classroom, and it helped spread respectfulness throughout the room. He knew that he could say anything he wanted as long as it was in a way that showed respect towards others. I also started listening and talking more to Ethan with empathy. Working on Ethan's anger management, I told him that I had many moments when I was also very upset with others, sometimes with myself, and this was a very human thing. Some people have it more than others. The art is not being lost in your upset and harming others. Some days it was very simple for Ethan to not become upset, but at the end he was someone who could easily get upset, especially when things went differently than planned. To help him and myself, I gave him this option: "Whenever you are upset, it's okay. Just walk to the hallway to create some space and time for yourself. Whenever I am finished with giving instructions, I'll come to you and you can say whatever is going on." While Ethan was growing rapidly, I realized that meeting someone at a space where he is a unique person makes people feel valued, appreciated, accepted and allows the person to grow. Isn't that all what we want, to be accepted and have the possibility to be ourselves without being judged? The more I had one-on-one sessions with Ethan and meetings with Ethan's mother in the afternoons and even sometimes phone calls later in the evenings, Ethan started revealing other sides he had. He was incredibly smart and intelligent, and he had selective attention for everything to do with space and science. One day when talking about fast animals on Earth, I pointed out that the cheetah might be the fastest animal. Ethan commented that might not be true, it might be a bird, the peregrine falcon.

While I studied books about the behavior of people and created automatic assumptions about people with special needs, I learned that my judgement didn't fit the actual person. The only truth for me was Ethan's self and his uniqueness. Didn't our uniqueness make us all equal? Often in Istanbul, when I woke up, tired or not tired, I created a new mantra: "Today there is a chance that one person will change your life forever."

4. RESISTANCE

I am not I.
I am this one
walking beside me whom I do not see,
whom at times I manage to visit,
and whom at other times I forget;
who remains calm and silent while I talk,
and forgives, gently, when I hate,
who walks where I am not,
who will remain standing when I die.

— Juan Ramón Jiménez

Having traveled for almost three weeks in China and South Korea, I was looking forward to visiting the Zen gardens, eating great local food and meeting locals in Japan. During my flight to Osaka I read about Japanese living in harmony, their willingness to live a simple life, and the importance of kindness and integrity. After a short visit to Osaka I headed to Kyoto, the ancient capital of Japan. I was pretty tired of traveling for three weeks and was looking forward to getting a nice rest at the hostel.

Entering the hostel, I saw a beautifully decorated wall with Japanese pottery in various colors and shapes next to the staircase leading upstairs. I climbed the stairs slowly to the reception, admiring the beauty. Although I was traveling on a low budget, I resisted using a backpack and chose instead a stylish trolley-sized suitcase which I maneuvered to the reception waiting area. There I stood opposite the owner who was behind a counter. He welcomed me with a gentle voice and bow, while his eyes were looking downward, and his arms were straight at his sides. His bow was truly felt, encompassing his presence, and respect and tolerance flew from him. While checking in with this man, I got to know his name which was Kazuya. He told me that there was something wrong with my booking. I had booked a four day stay in the female dormitory, but there wasn't a bed available for the first two days. Kazuya offered me a bed in the mixed dormitory, which meant my biggest nightmare—sleeping in a room with men I did not know.

Coming from an immigrant family with Turkish heritage, since the age of twelve I had never walked in underwear through the house. Underwear was set as the most extreme form, I never wore sleeveless tops or shorts above my knees. Moving out of my parents' home made me more self-reflective and conscious of which clothes I would like to wear. Even though I started liking to wear more fashionable clothes, I was still a prudish girl who didn't walk around a room in my underwear or wear a bikini at the beach or swimming pool. I didn't feel comfortable being naked or nearly naked. Over the years I taught myself to be comfortable wearing a bikini, but I still resisted walking around in front of others in my underwear. Sometimes I was very critical of myself and at the same time ashamed of being prudish. I also thought it was a conservative thing. Being raised in the West, I initially made the assumption that all Westerners were progressive, and I thought people would judge me for being conservative. And now being in this hostel in Kyoto, Kazuya was recommending I stay and sleep in a mixed room where males were present. I could feel that I was anxious about this offer and my building anxiety was only the tip of the iceberg. My whole being tensed up and I realized that protecting myself and my body from others was important to me, especially when being viewed by men. Physical contact with men meant for me not a casual thing, yet a sacred activity. While living abroad, I tried to get over this sacred idea in my head, but I couldn't change it because I realized that I didn't want to. Yet, I didn't want the sacred activity of physical contact to go together with anxiety to protect my body.

The more anxious I became, the more my fear took over and I started becoming a person ruled by her anxiety. I was upset with Kazuya and my voice got higher in volume. I remember the sentences I used, *"I made a reservation. I paid for it. I am the customer. I need to be treated well, you have to solve the problem."* Any sentence I used was in the direction to get what I wanted and where I could be in my comfort zone and I didn't care if Kazuya was out of his comfort zone. From my side there was nothing in the direction of tolerance, understanding or empathy. No, I only wanted Kazuya to understand me, tolerate me, and find a solution so I didn't have to sleep in the same room with men.

Kazuya started apologizing a few times, I heard him but I wasn't actively listening. I was only listening for my own sake and what he was saying wasn't what I wanted to hear. I was looking to find a solution for myself, staying in this hostel in the female dormitory. I kept going with my provoking words until suddenly, as if someone slapped my face, I stopped for a moment and really looked at myself and my attitude. Something had cracked or changed inside of me. I saw myself as a self-centered kiddo who didn't see the person in front of me, Kazuya. In a split second, I started seeing my own behavior, being selfish and trying to only win for myself and trying to resist something I didn't want to feel. The blaming towards Kazuya was merely due to an insecurity and something that I was resisting deeply in myself. While I knew I was better than this, I realized only knowing that I was better than this wasn't enough, this moment I had to practice it. Therefore, I started sincerely apologizing to Kazuya. The sentence that I used was in the direction of, *"I am really sorry that this happened and my way of handling it."* While I initially separated myself from Kazuya, a space in my heart was expanding. I felt the connection to another human being in front of me. After my self-centered behavior I eventually realized there had been a mistake, not knowing where it came from, the booking site or the administration of this hostel. There was a mistake and the owner was really sorry! That's it, full stop. I could choose to see it as I was right, which I did initially and served my ego. But by giving up looking for *"I am right"* and surrendering to the situation, I could connect with him and allow the issue to solve itself. I apologized and he apologized again. But words weren't needed anymore. I smiled, he did as well. At the moment I chose to relax and surrender to the situation, I was able to connect and see the kindness of the person in front of me. Even though I could go to another hostel with a bed in a female dormitory, I ultimately decided to stay. I stayed in the mixed dormitory, worked through my fear, and what a stay it was— I loved it!

5. KINDNESS

Even after all this time the sun never says to the earth,
'You owe me.'
Look what happens with a love like that.
It lights the whole sky.

— Hafiz

I was only twenty-four years old when I moved to a magical city where East meets West, Istanbul. As my father used to exaggerate there were more than seventy-seven different ethnicities in Istanbul. Each street in Istanbul seemed to represent a different culture, making me think I was entering a different world on each street. Religious, non-religious, creatives, fortune tellers, artists, Western, Eastern, intellectuals, illiterates, and more were all living here. The Bosporus Bridge was like a symbol of East meeting West. On one side there was Europe and on the other side Asia. Every morning I traveled from my apartment in Europe to my work in Asia, moving daily between East and West. Because I grew up in the Netherlands with most Eastern immigrants and native Dutch people, it made me used to moving between East and West, not in geographical terms but in my mind and behavior, because I learned from a young age to constantly adapt to the environment and people. My family always welcomed unannounced visitors in our house and shared food with them, but I was rarely spontaneously invited to my Dutch friends' houses to have dinner. It was usually planned in order to make sure there was enough food prepared for everyone. Collective thinking was prized in my household over individuality. But at school I learned to recognize myself as an individual and say my individual opinions freely.

At work at an international school on the Asian side of Istanbul, there was a young lady in her early twenties sitting in front of me at a round table in the canteen. She had a blazer and some smart pants, I believed maybe to fit in her role as a teacher. At first it was difficult to understand her native American-English accent, but I connected to her anyway. Her story was one of a kind. The moment I met her she had just married a few weeks ago to her husband from Turkey. She lost her heart to somebody and took a leap based on faith. Mary was from the woods of Virginia in the United States. She was a great person with an open heart. When she had just moved to Istanbul, she had made the intention to adapt to the Turkish culture and the family culture of her husband. This was definitely not an easy task for Mary. Whereas I was struggling between an Eastern and more Western identity, she chose to live in Istanbul in a very different culture than where she came from. She started living in a neighborhood where people were not really familiar with Mary's culture and had strong opinions about what life should be like. This was very different from the culture where Mary was brought up. Mary deliberately chose to be comfortably uncomfortable. For instance, Mary was also a competitive runner since she was a child. But running in Istanbul was initially difficult for her because there wasn't really an outside running culture in her neighborhood. Running drew attention and even walking on the street was not something she was used to because in Virginia she drove everywhere. However, Mary didn't give up and started running on the treadmill at a nearby gym.

This young lady didn't connect with many people but the people she connected with loved her. Mary was authentic, she was true to herself and true to others; she wasn't pretentious. Mary chose to find joy in all dimensions of her life, no matter what comments might have been said around her, no matter what happened at work, no matter if water got splashed on her due to heavy rains in the Istanbul streets. I could feel from time-to-time Mary was struggling to adapt and live in Istanbul. Her ideal world would be living in Virginia or any other place in the United States which was her comfort zone. Mary was a quiet and especially gentle person. She didn't talk that much, but at times when she chose to talk, her words were chosen carefully and deliberately in a gentle way. She was definitely different from me. Back then I loved small talks and Mary did the right amount of talk at the right time. She knew how to use the right leverage at the right time. I loved going out to fancy places and constantly meeting new people because I thought this was something cool. When I was dancing late into the night in these fancy bars or clubs, Mary was sleeping in her bed or writing stories, watching movies and having quality time with her cat. In those times, for me constantly meeting new people, having chats here and there and being especially liked and recognized were very important to me, but Mary was more timid and carefully chose the people she met and talked to. I also felt that she didn't care that much of what people thought about her. She just did her thing, but at the same time she was extremely respectful to her surroundings and didn't want to offend anyone.

Even though we had our differences, Mary and I found a ground where we could meet and connect. Somehow our hearts melted into each other. Mary was a big giver, she gave her time, she gave things in materials, she gave emotional support, and it always looked like Mary did this from the bottom of her heart. Mary was like a newborn in my eyes, so innocent and pure. For example, Mary rarely judged or commented on other people and never said something bad, even though you could feel at times she was uncomfortable with that person. There was so much that I could learn from Mary. I never heard Mary complaining about someone or something, even though life was at times tough for her, she found a ground where she found joy. So Mary was this kind of person that was all in the service of others and never complained.

2014 - Charlottesville, Virginia, United States

A few years later Mary left Istanbul and moved back to Virginia. Since I was already visiting the East Coast of the United States, she invited me to celebrate Thanksgiving together with her family in Charlottesville, Virginia. Although I only celebrated Thanksgiving earlier with my international students and colleagues at the international school in Istanbul, I didn't know all the details. I only knew that people from the United States were being thankful for the things they had in their lives. Most of them were thanking their family, but also the opportunities they had in life, health, friends, their jobs and even the food they could eat.

On the way to the big house of Mary's grandparents, I felt that I was in a fascinating place. The mysterious big house was in a forest and the only thing I saw was yellow, brown and orange leaves. The whole forest was kind of a dreamland. The trees gave themselves over to nature, letting their leaves fall with huge trust that soon they would grow again, trusting that spring would come, but by only letting go first. After arriving together with Mary and her husband at Mary's grandparent's house in the middle of the forest, we were welcomed by the whole family: Mary's grandparents,

parents and brothers. At the time, I thought this could only happen in a Turkish family but the dining table was huge and on each spot there were pies, cakes, soups, salads not known dishes, and a turkey that came cooked from the oven. Sitting around the table, the conversation flowed freely while we tasted the delicious food.

On the way back to Mary's house we stopped at a coffee shop to get coffee. To my surprise, for the first time in my life I saw a coffee shop drive-through. I only knew the drive through from one of the fast-food chains in Alkmaar, the Netherlands where I used to often go with my brother and father. We could stop by car and get an ice cream through the window. Yet, now here in Virginia, there was a coffee shop drive through which I had never seen before. While waiting behind a huge car, I was already thinking of what I wanted to drink and knew I would get a latte as always. When arriving at the screen we ordered what we wanted and the barista told us that the people in the car in front of us who had already left had paid our order forward. I was so surprised and at the same time in awe. It wasn't just the coffee but this kind act from strangers that empowered my heart and made me want to reciprocate such a kind act as well. I knew I liked giving, but I couldn't ever remember giving to someone without knowing who that person was and I was usually expecting a return in favor...

2018 - Kyoto, Japan

I got my chance to reciprocate that specific kindness at the coffee shop drive-through in Charlottesville, Virginia a few years later when I was in Japan for a second time. While walking in one of the local markets in the suburbs of Kyoto I saw a bouquet with pink flowers. I just loved the way they were. But I was on a bike on my way to the botanical garden in Kyoto and I thought I wouldn't be able to carry the flowers with me during my visit. Then I remembered the kind act from the people in the drive-through at the coffee shop during Thanksgiving in the United States and I decided to buy the flowers anyways and make someone else happy. When walking with a big smile on my face I saw an old lady, whom I assumed might be around eighty years old. By saying *"Sumimasen,"* (used in Japanese to get attention) I stopped her and with body language gave the flowers to her. The lady turned it down. Being a little discouraged, I cycled my way to the botanical garden. I decided to go on intuition and knew exactly that I would go to the right place. It was around thirty-five degrees Celsius and I was sweating in the streets of Kyoto. Although it was hot, it was still peaceful. In one of the streets, I discovered a shop that was selling sushi and candies wrapped in traditional Japanese wrapping paper. I stopped by and reached out to give the flowers to the lady selling the candies. The lady put a big smile on her face and said, *"Arigato,"* (thank you) with a gentle bow. A sweet kindness was felt throughout my whole body.

6. JUDGEMENT

The wound is the place where the light enters you.

— Jalal ad-Din Muhammad Rumi

Here I was, feeling numb and sick, lying in a hospital bed in Denmark, not knowing I would end up like this and worried about how I would make it out of this situation.

The beginning of my illness started in the bus on the way back to Aarhus from Brande. I was at a company training in a small town called Brande in Denmark. Each time I was in this small town, I thought there were more sheep than people. It was always quiet, serene and green in all directions with a few houses. The training in the morning was followed by the usual excellent company prepared lunch, which always satisfied my gluttony. After lunch, in the company bus to a hotel in Aarhus, I became nauseous so I rushed to the bathroom on the bus. A combination of motion sickness and overeating resulted in having to empty my stomach in the bathroom. Going back to my seat, I felt very sick and while there wasn't any food left in my stomach I could feel that it was upset and very bloated.

Having survived the bus ride and arrived at the hotel in Aarhus, I checked into my shared room. The room contained two beds that were eighty centimeters in width with only enough space between them for a very small night table. When I saw the room I became anxious because I knew there was a lot of flatulence in my body and I somehow needed to get it out. But being in the same room with my colleague made me shy and try to keep the flatulence in and this resulted in an expansion of the bloating in my stomach. Additionally, on top of my stomach woes, I was worried I might accidentally kick my colleague in my sleep because of the lack of space between the beds. Altogether, the first night was spent troubled by anxiety and an increasingly bloated stomach.

Back at the training session, now in the office in Aarhus, I hoped that somehow my bloated stomach could lighten up. After compulsively going to the bathroom the flatulence was insistent and even burping was something I wasn't able to do. The more I tried to pass the gas, the more my stomach seemed to expand. At the end of the training day, where I was anything but present, I went to my friend's house, Kevser's, instead of my hotel room. I was fearful of being judged by my colleague in the hotel room and that was the last thing I wanted to experience at the moment. Since I was very comfortable and close to Kevser, and most importantly knew that she wouldn't judge me on anything, it was better for me to go to her house where I knew I could burp and attempt to get rid of the flatulence whenever I needed. In the bedroom, we were literally waiting for my body to pass wind so I could feel better. Kevser and I had never been so thrilled before until when my body passed a little flatulence, as silly as it seemed.

The next day, after passing wind a few times somehow my tummy kept its bloated form so I stayed back in the hotel and didn't go to the office due to increasing stomach cramps. As much as I was glad that I was alone in the hotel room and could pass any flatulence when I needed to, physically I couldn't and my tummy kept expanding. I had landed many times before in various countries in the hospital due to tummy aches. After many checks they couldn't find anything and almost all doctors thought that the possible cause might be stress. This time, I was hesitant to go to the hospital again for the same things and receive the same reaction from doctors as before, which I was actually fed up with. After the ever increasing pressure, bloating, and expanding pain in my abdomen, feeling lonely, and pitying myself in the hotel room, I called a cab and went to the hospital. I waited an hour in the waiting room, the pain and feeling of being a victim increasing with every minute, only to later leave the hospital with an injection in my butt, which would hopefully result in allowing the flatulence to leave my body. The doctor, like before, sounded to me as if on repeat, and stated that there was nothing visible or apparent for causing the pain in my abdomen.

Back in the hotel room when it was dark and the sun had already set, I laid down and tried to sleep, still with a lot of aches. My colleague in the same room didn't arrive, yet my friends Zafer and Adam, who were staying next door in the hotel, checked on me from time-to-time and made me feel safe by saying that I could knock on the wall in case something happened. This kindness from them made me feel very safe and I could feel that I actually wasn't lonely, someone else was thinking of me. It was hard to sleep at night, with many turns in bed and thoughts in my mind. I remember very well: I was alone, my colleague still wasn't in the room and it was just before midnight, I turned one more time, trying to get comfortable until all of a sudden a pain erupted like someone stabbed my lower belly with a knife, just a little bit on the right side, exactly on the edge of my underwear. The pain was unbearable. Something inside my lower tummy was shaking and causing a pain that I had never felt before. After this feeling it felt like there was a kind of ball radiating pain in all directions. I woke up and knocked with all my power on the wall behind the bed, desperately hoping Zafer and Adam would come. All my attention and energy went to this pain, I was getting weaker with each second but kept knocking on the wall as hard as my body allowed. Alternating between feeling pain, knocking on the wall and breathing I found myself desperately leaning against the wall until I heard Adam at my door. Trying to put myself together I limped to the door, opened it, and yelled in panic to call an ambulance. Meanwhile, Zafer got the emergency personnel from the reception up to the third floor. Adam stood in front of me, held me and tried to make me walk. My voice became louder, my speaking quicker. I was in the grip of a large panic. Sweat dripped off my face, my entire body was perspiring. Sweat was falling from my hair, forehead and even my pyjama bottom and top were wet with sweat. We had to walk to the elevator. The ten meter walk to the elevator felt like running a marathon with blisters and aches and no energy left for even one more step forward. Having spent all my energy walking to the elevator and going down, I couldn't walk anymore and sat on a couch in the hallway just outside of the elevator because the pain was unbearable. Adam stayed with me the whole time and wanted to make sure I was okay but I really wasn't. Within a few minutes the ambulance came but it felt like hours. They placed me in a wheelchair and we exited the hotel. Next to the hotel was a bar and everyone was looking at me, making me feel even worse. I never liked eyes on me and also this time I hated it, eyes on me. I was in my pyjamas, looking really sick and people were standing and looking at me. When entering the ambulance Zafer and Adam were constantly with me. The nurse in the ambulance was doing many things which I can't remember and while he was busy with all these things he asked me many questions. Meanwhile, when the nurse was injecting a needle into my hand, I could feel that the pain was slowly fading away and I got with each second more relaxed. It was morphine. Despite never liking drugs nor ever using any illicit or hard drugs, with the idea of even using drugs making me feel bad, this time it was something I loved. I was kind of like "give me more" because all this panicking, pain, and anxiety slowly started to fade away.

Arriving at the hospital, the doctors thought there was something going on in the area of my uterus and decided to send me to the gynecology department. Being prude was in my whole being, especially among men. Yet when pain crossed paths with being prudish, I felt that I had to let go of being prudish. I was sitting on the gynecology chair and different doctors came and looked at what was going on. The only thing they "saw" through the ultrasound monitor were some cysts around my uterus. This was supposed to be a normal thing in my age. While the blood tests showed an increasing CRP level and an infection in my body, the doctors thought that beside the cysts I was suffering from constipation. They gave me some medicine to make my bowels work despite the fact that there was already a lot of movement in my bowels, yet the flatulence didn't come out. The nurse also told me that I could go home or I could stay in the hospital for the night. Of course I wanted to stay in the hospital and not the hotel room with the eighty centimeter bed and being fearful of passing flatulence next to my colleague in addition to worrying if the unbearable pain might start up again after the morphine left my system. After getting more morphine I tried to sleep in the hospital room but I still had a lot of bowel movements going on.

Waking up the next morning, I heard from the nurse that another doctor was going to see me. When the door of the hospital room opened, this amazingly good looking guy with a nerdy look entered the room. He was tall, had dark hair, alabaster white skin and glasses over his brown eyes. His voice was calm and he definitely looked intelligent to me. Despite all the physical and psychological pain I was in, I thought it wasn't a good time for him to be here in this room because I was having my worst look ever. With guys I found good looking, I always felt that I needed to look extremely good, otherwise I would feel less than them and think I wasn't attractive. Here I was in my oversized hospital pyjamas, like grandmother pyjamas, my hair loose but going in all directions, and this amazingly good looking young doctor. After introducing himself, Fred, the good looking doctor asked with a gentle calm voice to show him my abdomen. A voice in my head was resisting to show this good looking doctor my sick body, but I also didn't want to die and felt that I had to. I actually would have hoped in a life outside of the hospital that he would like me. The doctor put his fingers on my tummy and did a variety of checks. I saw him looking at my red polished toes and even in physical pain I was joyful that something at least looked good. I was in unbearable pain and aware that I was still up for approval from this good looking doctor. I was even surprised how seeking approval from someone was so important to me in a situation where I had experienced the heaviest physical pain. When Fred started putting a bit more pressure on one side of my tummy I screamed and hit his hand. It was only a reflex to the extreme pain I felt. In panic of what I had done, I apologized to Fred for my reaction. With a calm voice he said that it was okay and kept checking my abdomen. After he was finished with the check he said that again another doctor, the third doctor for me now in my short stay, would see me together with him. So again we headed to the gynecology chair next door and here I was in extra large hospital underwear, sitting in the chair while a female doctor in her fifties and good looking Fred discussed what was going on. Being fearful, I tried to understand the look on their faces while they were discussing something in Danish which I didn't understand at all, my mind was making so much noise: am I having cancer, is there another illness, what is going on, tell me please! While an extreme natural curiosity in me made me gain knowledge easily and learn, I felt frightened when I didn't know something I wanted to know. I had always been very scared of the unknown and nervous about the future. Maybe that's why I had been suffering from stomach aches since childhood...

While being in the gynecology chair additional new blood tests showed a huge increase of the infection in my body. Both gynecologists told me that I had to undergo surgery, if possible immediately, and they had to take out the cysts they saw next to my uterus which had been considered by the doctors a "normal" thing just the day before. Since both gynecologists made clear that this is actually not a general process, the surgery decision was quickly made from the quickly increasing infection in my body. I started crying and thought that moment I would die. Panic took over. I was not a doctor, I believed that the doctors would know a lot, but this time I was sure that there was something else than the cyst. Staying in the hospital with extreme cramps in my tummy and many bowel movements without being able to go to the bathroom told me something else was wrong. I only wanted to call my good friends and talk to them and cry out my anxiety and tell them I loved them so much. I suffered extremely from the idea that I would die. As much as I wanted to have my family beside me and even only hear their voices on the phone, I also didn't want to call them, especially my mother, because I didn't want them to panic.

In no time my traineeship company's colleagues came to see me and led me to the surgery room. In only two years time I believed that I didn't belong to their friendship. I found it difficult to connect to them. Most of them were younger than me and had different interests. Even though I believed that different interests shouldn't matter to connect to human beings, it was difficult for me to connect to them. Also, the fact that I was in the traineeship group and was kind of obliged to connect to them, made me feel pushed and made it harder for me to connect to them. I never felt like doing things if I felt pushed into something. I thought they didn't like me and saw me as someone from another planet. Yet, I never knew that I was the one creating this distance between them and myself. Since the beginning, I had been judgmental about them. I had already made a conclusion about them without really exploring who they really were. Since I was one of the oldest trainees, I assumed that I was more experienced, which meant believing I knew more and thus was better than them. I believed that wisdom was based on age, studying, and work experience. While I thought I was wiser than them and judged them harshly, I didn't allow myself to see them for who they were. But this time the presence of the people I had judged was truly felt by me in the hospital room. They took the time from their very busy final project and came to support me. They called and constantly sent messages asking how I was. At a moment of panic, when I thought that I would die in the surgery room, the people who surrounded me were these colleagues whom I had chosen to not connect to over the last two years. The connection that moment, just before the surgery, had a strength I had never felt before. These were the people that were with me at one of the most painful and fearful moments of my life. Zafer and Adam, who were my saving guardians starting in the hotel until the last day in the hospital. And then there was this girl Kevser, who became a model example of someone who offered selfless support. Kevser and I met each other on our training trip to China in the airplane. Initially, we were not a big fan of each other, actually we didn't like each other. We both had judgments of each other. Getting back from the China trip, Kevser and I weren't in touch until a common friend of ours recommended to get to know each other better. When we gave each other the chance to do that, I started loving Kevser. Kevser is this person with a house where everyone is welcome, regardless of your beliefs in life. Kevser is this person that thinks in terms of good things about people. She became my sister, a present from the Universe. A sister that I thought I didn't ask for, yet I might have done it. Isn't the rule of the Universe that no question is unheard and no question goes unanswered?

After being led to the surgery room by people I had judged initially and then got support from, I went under general anesthesia for the first time and remember waking up to seeing a catheter connected to my body. The surgery resulted in a different outcome as my intuition forecasted. Doctors came across my inflamed and later ruptured appendix which made me suffer and at the same time made me start seeing people beyond my own judgements. Both my appendix and judgements were removed. The person I was before the surgery transformed into another one.

7. AUTHENTICITY

Carry your heart through this world like a life-giving sun.

— Hafiz

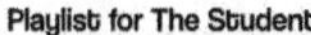

The last apartment I lived in when living in Istanbul was in a narrow street. It was a charming apartment on the sixth rooftop floor, and this apartment had a spectacular view of the stars at night. When I was tired and sitting in a chair next to the window, I would watch the stars and Istanbul from my small window. Actually, I was only partly watching Istanbul, the thing I was really watching was the Universe which turned into darkness, away from the man-made lights. I was interested in the stars, I still am. Since I was a child I dreamed of a higher power being in the sky and watching me back when I watched the sky, night or day—it didn't matter. The stars were always beautiful and at the same time magical. I kind of kept my breath in and only watched the stars and the moon. I could feel that I was one with the sky and the sky was one with me. I was watching the night and the night was watching me.

The narrow street was exactly at the edge of a fancy neighborhood known as Nişantaşı, but this narrow street wasn't a fancy street at all. When walking towards the narrow street from main Nişantaşı the street went downhill, out of sight of the restaurants and cafes, boutique shops, and cosmetic clinics. I was told by my neighbors that this narrow street and the area around it except Nişantaşı had been a place of poverty until the 1980s. While it was the 21st century when I was living there and not the 1980s, people in this area were generally more economically impoverished than people in the main area of Nişantaşı, which was only one hundred meters away. Most men in this narrow street and the surrounding area worked very physical labor jobs whereas men in the main area of Nişantaşı worked office jobs. Women living on this narrow street were mostly homemakers and knitted some slippers and decorations for the home or to sell, whereas most women in the other Nişantaşı spent their days in offices and afterwards might drink and dine at one of the fancy restaurants nearby.

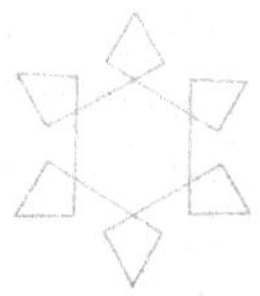

This narrow street had hardly any light at night. The dim light on this street made me feel scared sometimes when I arrived home after joining a party in one of the bars and clubs of Istanbul. When I lived in Istanbul I partied a lot and believed back then that it gave me comfort. At any party I could forget about the struggles of the day, meet some new and interesting people, drink and dance my struggles of life away. When it was Thursday I already started thinking about which parties I could join on Friday and Saturday night. I loved the dancing part of parties where I could embrace my body. Although I never was a big drinker of alcohol, I started consuming it to fit into the social norms and also to get comfortable with myself and my body. After my first few experiences, I realized I was getting drunk with three drinks and that's why I often stopped drinking while having my third drink or I didn't order a third drink at all. I was often ambivalent about controlling a situation. If I wanted to be in full control I didn't drink or only drank one glass. This happened often in situations where I didn't feel comfortable and many men were present. It could be just a regular bar or club where I had felt many eyes on me, making me immediately feel intimidated. I somehow believed that I had to protect myself and this was accomplished by being sober. When deliberately wanting to be "out of control" and be more comfortable around people, I would drink more to get tipsy and sometimes drunk. Those situations occurred usually when I was with my close friends or had a crush on a guy. When I was tipsy I believed my ego boosted and I thought I could do anything and nothing would really happen to me. So I am not sure if it was me or the alcohol itself that was the courageous one, the one who could step up to a man, start a conversation, and even tell him that I was interested in him.

While visiting bars and clubs gave me comfort, the comfort and additional love I received from a woman who lived on this narrow street was different. She has an uncommon name, a name I had never heard of before, Marziye. I undoubtedly started calling her *Marziye Abla*. *Abla* means older sister in Turkish. In the culture I grew up, I learned to call an older Turkish woman *Abla* and an older Turkish man *Abi* as a sign of respect. While showing respect to her by calling her Marziye Abla, I also felt more connected and close to her. Abla is a word still used by traditional and modern Turks in Turkey and abroad. Even though I was living in a modern neighborhood in Istanbul, I absolutely loved being traditional at times. While I was born and raised in the West, when being in the West my heart used to be in the East and usually when I was in the East my mind was in the West. Having such a connection with this middle-aged lady and calling her Abla gave me more than comfort, it created a warm and deep connection. Marziye Abla wasn't a stranger to me anymore, she became someone very close. She was from a little village in Konya, a major city in the south-western edge of Central Turkey. She was married to Mehdi, who used to farm in a little village in Konya. Together with her husband, Marziye Abla had moved to this narrow street in Nişantaşı many years ago. Every single person on the narrow street knew her. This small and a bit chubby lady possessed a big heart. She was generous and liked giving without expecting, liked helping without wanting anything in return, and liked listening without expecting to be listened to. She simply seemed joyous to be in the service of others. These attributes of her had an enormous effect on me. Although I was taught by my parents and teachers to be generous, help others and listen to others, I almost always expected something in return.

Marziye Abla once told me, *"You live here and we, all the people living in this narrow street, are your family. If something ever happens, no matter what, no matter what time, you can knock on our door, if you aren't able to knock you make a sound, yell, say something and we are outside at that moment with you, next to you."* I have never been that comfortable with darkness, but coming home late at night or early in the morning when it was dark in this tiny narrow street made me feel at ease. I used to think it was the parties I attended in fancy places that gave me comfort, but this time it was Marziye Abla with her presence. I truly felt as if I had a big family—the whole street—because of her. Marziye Abla selflessly gave me comfort, protection, a feeling of belonging and I believed that she didn't expect anything in return.

As much as it was enjoyable to teach students at an international school in Istanbul, after a long day I often entered the narrow street tired and without any energy left. Entering the narrow street made me smile because Marziye Abla was at her window. She sort of had a membership at her window. She loved it, gazing at people, talking to them. There wasn't a day that Marziye Abla didn't ask from her second-story window if I had food at home. Regardless of my answer, she would put in her straw basket sometimes *börek* (Turkish savory pastry), sometimes eggs, sometimes another dish and would lower the basket to give to me. Some places in Turkey, especially in Anatolia (Asian Turkey), they use a straw basket to put things in and send the basket down from a tall building to give a person below its contents.

Marziye Abla mostly smiled and never complained. Even the days I knew she wasn't feeling well due to hardships in her life, she still smiled. One day, Marziye Abla was as usual at her window. She had been hospitalized and she chose to initially not tell me and genuinely asked how I was and was more interested in me than her illness. Her husband Mehdi was usually sitting outside in a simple chair with a glass of Turkish tea after a day of hard work carrying boxes from the business owners of the textile industry. He usually invited me to also drink a glass with him which I usually did. The boiling hot tea in the small tulip-shaped glass was accompanied by chats about Mehdi Abi's life back in the little village in Konya, his life now and his dreams. I loved listening to him and getting to know him better. Sometimes I sat with him for hours, drinking many glasses of tea, listening to him talk and occasionally asking him questions because I was so interested in his life, the way he thought, the motivations behind his actions in life. He seemed extraordinary to me.

On one hot summer day when I entered the narrow street I saw Marziye Abla and other neighbors putting together many plastic tables and chairs, bringing food and drinks to the tables. I asked what was going to happen and then one of the neighbors invited me to join them for the Iftar dinner which is the evening meal at every sunset during the holy month of Ramadan. As I climbed the stairs to my apartment, great memories of Iftar dinners back home when I was a child floated through my mind. Paradoxically, I had stopped fasting when I had moved to Istanbul. But I was excited to be participating in the Iftar dinner again, so I changed my clothes from shorts to long pants and another decent top, then went back down to the narrow street. All women, men, and children were sitting at a very long table made up of many tables. Every woman had made her best dish and the men had helped to arrange the tables and put them together. There was a beautiful smile on most people's faces. These people were willing to take actions to improve the general welfare of the people living in this narrow street. I could feel the bonding of all these people together. There was sincerity, genuine regard, and love. People were ready to practice for most of them a religious act and for me a spiritual act. Sitting there, tears of love welled in my eyes, tears of feeling love among people. When the sun set, people were ready to pray, pray to God and show gratitude for togetherness, for being alive and for the food. Every single person at my table wanted to make sure I had enough food and was doing well. They were so very interested in me as a person, who I was, what I did, why I chose to live in Istanbul, and why I even chose to come to the Iftar dinner.

At the table where I was sitting I met a calm middle-aged man who held prayer beads in his right hand. His name was Önder but he told me that everyone calls him "Önder Baba" and I could call him that, too. *Önder Baba* means "father Önder." Calling him Önder Baba put me at ease and I felt connected to this man. When he listened to me he was listening with a focus and each time intensified his listening even more. When he looked at me, he was present. At the end of our conversation, he said, "Don't forget two things in life, it will bring you peace." His two things were sentences from the poet and mystic Yunus Emre, "*Love the created for the Creator's sake,*" and "*There are eyes which don't see, but there are no hearts which don't see.*" With this said, I knew and could feel that he loved me because of the Creator and the sake of my being. He loved me because we were one.

Prior to living in this narrow street, appreciating others that I didn't know or weren't connected to and even people that weren't good to me was a challenging task. I believed in doing good to others who were also good to me and this was something I did easily. Living in this narrow street at the charming apartment situated on the sixth rooftop floor, it brought much more than a spectacular view of the stars at night. It also came with the people I met in this narrow street who taught me to give, to appreciate, and to expect nothing in return.

Memories of Iftar dinner
During the holy month of Ramadan, Muslims fast between sunrise and sunset. They make sure to abstain from eating, drinking and intimate relations from sunrise until sundown. Fasting taught me self-discipline, self-control and empathy for those who are less fortunate. Additionally, by resetting my mind, body and soul during fasting I became closer to a higher power. Ramadan brings a deep sense of gratitude to me. Ever since I was six years old until I left the Netherlands for Istanbul, I fasted during the month of Ramadan. My mother woke us up before sunrise and the table was always packed with our favorite dishes. Yet, despite all of our favorite foods, we couldn't really eat a lot. I remember waking up with one eye still closed and eating some homemade toasted bread with butter and Dutch cheese on it. Even with bits in my mouth I was walking to the bathroom to brush my teeth, drink water and go immediately back to bed. Most evenings during Ramadan we were invited for "Iftar," a dinner at sunset, to my parent's friends or we would have guests over. Being very busy in the kitchen, warming up the food that my mother cooked and preparing the table, was one of the nicest moments of the day. Most people in the house were fasting and were very hungry. I could feel people's hunger, their waiting, the deep presence of gratitude and being together. I could feel what it meant to be hungry and at the same time what it meant to be disciplined. After making sure the sun set we broke our fast with a little date and a glass of water. That moment was my most grateful moment. I prayed by thanking for not only food, but bringing us together with gratitude.

8. PAST & FUTURE

Be fearless.
Fly anywhere.
Shed off your thoughts.
Do anything.
Whatever your soul desires.
Fearless is nothing about
Saying that you are not fearful.
Or pretending that you are fearless.
Fearless is all about vulnerability.
Accept your fear.
Unfriend fear.
Befriend yourself.
Come back to your senses.

— ÖÖ

Playlist for The Student

I never expected to have a panic attack in a plane. I was at Billund Airport in Denmark and I had a flight to Helsinki via Stockholm. The initial flight to Stockholm was going to take only fifty minutes. The weekend prior to my flight I had many cramps in my stomach. Even though I felt much better now, I was nervous and anxious about the possibility that I would get sick again and was hanging in the past experience. At the airport I decided to take some green juice and crackers. It was my first big meal I had eaten after suffering the whole weekend of stomach cramps and a constant urge to vomit. After my meal I started cueing to enter the plane. With entering the cue, I felt pressure in my stomach and kept burping for a couple of minutes, one after the other. As I couldn't stop burping, my mind started spinning. I thought that I was again going to have unstoppable stomach cramps but now I was on the plane. Right after this flight I had to take another plane and I was mightily concerned about my stomach and the gas constantly coming up my throat. I was extremely embarrassed about what people would think of me. Would they perceive me as weak? Would they think I am mentally ill? All these thoughts were rushing through my mind and I started creating a rising panic.

Right after entering the plane I sat immediately in my seat and felt as if I couldn't breathe, like I was almost going to choke. After noticing my tingling fingers and feeling lightheaded, initially with resistance I decided to tell the steward that I wasn't feeling well. She gave me water to drink but it didn't help. Also, she first offered and then moved me to a seat at the front of the plane but that didn't help either. At the moment I heard the motors of the plane turning on as a sign to be ready to leave the airport, my breath became short. In confusion, I immediately called the steward one more time and told her that I didn't want to fly but the airplane had already started leaving the gate and getting ready for takeoff. I had thoughts passing through my mind that I would die in the air while flying. I didn't understand what was happening to me. I had flown many times since I was seven years old. Together with my own confusion I saw a confused steward asking me if this was my first time flying. While the drama I was unconsciously creating worked out and became bigger, I got a lot of attention. After the stewards' quick phone call with the staff, immediately and unexpectedly, one of the pilots stopped the plane on the tarmac and walked over to me and asked if I really didn't want to fly. Seeing the concern and at the same time care in his eyes, he mentioned that the plane would go back to the gate if my answer was in the direction that I didn't want to fly. Confused and as scared as I was, my head kept spinning and thoughts raced through my mind: What if something happens to me in the plane and I would die without having a doctor at my side? What are the pilots, stewards and passengers thinking of me? They might think she's just a fearful person, which was exactly what I didn't want them to think of me. I believed that I had to be the fearless girl, who was in fact very fearful but never wanted to show anyone. I thought that I had to be fearless, courageous and everything but weak. This conviction was something I had kept with me since childhood. As it served me well for many things, there were many moments that it started impeding me. I started finding it difficult to show my true self, the fearless but also fearful girl. In the confusion of two strong emotions that overtook me, not wanting to die and not wanting to be recognized as a weak person, I said that I was ready to fly. With those words, the pilot went back and turned on the motors of the plane for the second time. Witnessing my panic and suffering, a young woman in her early twenties just in the seat next to me started holding my hand and said, *'I will hold your hand and you will be okay.'* Grateful as I was to have her next to me, I started holding her hand very tight. A stream of feelings of comfort and safety started streaming from my hand through my whole body until a warm sensation reached my heart.

After this event in the plane I had to keep flying almost every week, due to my job, yet it was difficult to overcome my fear and anxiety to travel by plane each time, especially alone without anyone I knew. Before I even arrived at the airport my pulse would race, beads of perspiration would break out on my forehead, and my hands would become slick with sweat just anticipating the flight. I didn't want panic to take over or any of these thoughts about the past and future to come up. I wanted to be fearless—cool, calm, and collected. I was flying from the age of seven and thought, why should I stop flying because I once had a panic attack on a plane? Although it sounds brave and I continued to fly, I was extremely stressed during flights. The panic would build and build until it became a tidal wave that would crush and drown me. I strongly believed that something would happen to me. What if I had a panic attack like before? What if I had a heart attack in the plane and there was no one to save me? What if there was someone who wanted to hijack the plane? What if the plane all of a sudden started free-falling? I knew these were all scenarios my mind was creating because of the panic drowning out all reasonable thoughts about the past and future.

I was in the air once more and again trying to hide my fear when all of a sudden I was fed up with my panic and the drama around flying. I decided to confront and accept the panic face-on! So I turned to a lady next to me and told her what I was feeling, the anxiety of crashing and my fear of a panic attack. She told me that she believed that if by some chance a plane would crash you have no control over it, but it's up to you to decide how to spend your last hours and even minutes. You decide. I realized that I constantly worked on building up an anxiety with the start of thinking about a past experience, resulting in creating a huge distrust of flying. The anxiety and distrust increased even more when thoughts arose about a possible future experience: shame I would be recognized as someone weak by others. As I was ready to ultimately make a decision to enjoy the flight, slowly, I first started accepting any thought that passed through my mind and then slowly any emotion that passed through my body, fully surrendering to anything that could happen. And finally, I arrived back in my body, and into the present moment at peace.

9. PRIDE & EGO

You know what's right.
Just do right.
Right may not be expedient.
It may not be profitable.
But it will satisfy your soul.
It brings you the kind of protection,
that bodyguards can't give you.
Try to be all you can be.
To be the best human being you can be.
Try to be that in your church, in your temple.
Try to be that in your classroom.
Do it because it is right to do.

Take up the battle, take it up, it is yours, it is your life, this is your world.

— Maya Angelou

Living in Aarhus, Denmark meant short daylight hours in the winter and long summer days, with beautiful sunrises and sunsets each day. Every single morning when I biked to work I could see the beautiful sunrise and on the way back the setting sun. Different shades of blue, pink and yellow were part of the sky in Aarhus. Watching the sky made me feel like one with nature. Despite the breathtaking sunrise and sunsets, there were many moments when I felt lonely in Aarhus. I often stayed hidden in my room with my books, writing while avoiding the rain and freezing weather that I wasn't used to. For the first time, I was in a place where I felt like I didn't have any friends. I found it difficult to connect to other people around me. I hadn't experienced something like this since high school. So being very confused about the absence of connecting to people around me, which made me feel safe, comfortable, and sane, I kept reading and writing.

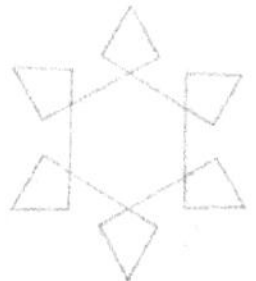

One day, when my friend Mette called and told me that she planned to visit, I was extremely thrilled. I literally jumped in the air due to my excitement. Mette was Danish and lived in another city in Denmark, yet we had met and became colleagues and friends back in Istanbul during our time living there. Because Mette and I didn't have a family while living in Istanbul, we became each other's family. Her plans to come visit meant the world to me, for a moment I would be with someone who knew me and that visit could be an escape from my loneliness. I arranged with Mette to come on a weekend because I knew my flatmate would be gone so she could stay in the unoccupied furnished room. A few days prior to Mette's arrival, my flatmate moved out, yet I noticed that she locked her room after moving out. My apartment had one entrance through the shared kitchen, a shared bathroom and two separate studio rooms where each person had a large room with a bed, dining table, TV, fridge and all other basic things you could find in an entire apartment except a bathroom and kitchen. We were able to lock the doors of the rooms, but my ex-flatmate and I actually never locked the doors. It was Friday, my friend was going to come on Saturday, and the door of the unoccupied room was now locked. Since the apartment was owned by the company I worked for, I decided to email the apartment manager and explain the situation and ask for the key to the unoccupied room. The apartment manager explained that I couldn't use the room because it didn't belong to me. Even after I explained that this was an exception because I rarely had a close friend visit me, and my friend really needed a separate room because she had a two year old son, the manager refused to allow me to use the space. Those were the rules and the apartment manager couldn't negotiate outside of the rigidity of those rules.

When hearing that I couldn't use the empty room in the apartment I was living in, I was furious. My anger took over all parts of my body. Whatever control I had before slipped away as quickly as water running through your hands. Who did the apartment manager think she was? I felt completely unsupported and this added another layer to me feeling lonely. I believed that the apartment manager was responsible for my loneliness which was quickly expanding to the outermost limits, by not allowing me to use the space across the hallway in the apartment I was living. In a very reactive mode, I decided to call the apartment manager. I was more than furious on the phone and started using provoking language with an increasingly loud tone by repeatedly mentioning she was wrong and didn't have the right to make me feel like this. Back then, I wasn't really aware that the only person who was making me furious was myself. The apartment manager was really only doing her job. The fact that she was doing her very best to arrange the room for me didn't matter. The only thing that really mattered was the way I treated her in the reactive mode I was in. After not making any progress about the room and causing the apartment manager to feel very bad about herself and my frustration expanding even more, I ended the call with a forceful "thank you," which meant everything but a real "thank you."

The next day my friend Mette came only for the day and didn't sleep over. Days passed and life went on, yet I still felt like I had a block in my spirit. I felt really bad but not because I didn't get the room. I felt bad because of how I had treated the apartment manager which was terrible. I had deliberately hurt another human being by allowing my emotions to take over. While knowing that this wasn't the right thing, I had still allowed it to happen. Maya Angelou's words were going through my mind: *"When you are taken over by your emotions, pause, stop, check back in with yourself and still do the right thing."* Intuitively, I knew there was a right thing for me to do. I genuinely wanted to apologize to the apartment manager. I wanted it so much but my pride and ego were stopping me as well as thoughts like, "You shouldn't say you are sorry," "You have a right to be upset with her," and many others. I knew those thoughts were only distracting me from the real thing: sincerely apologizing for my behavior. I decided to call the apartment manager and remembered using these sentences, "I am really sorry that I behaved to you very badly, you didn't deserve that. There is no excuse, what I did was wrong. I am truly sorry and won't do this again.

Reflecting back, I came to realize that when I didn't get what I wanted I became furious and was taken over by my emotions. I decided at that moment to blame and judge the apartment manager while showing irresponsible behavior only because there was something I was resisting: feeling lonely. Emotions come and go, they never stay forever and human beings make mistakes. By acknowledging the behavior I showed, it became more important for me to recognize how I would handle it. Even though my pride and ego weren't directing me to apologize, my heart wanted to restore my personal integrity by sincerely apologizing and promising myself to be more responsible next time, to pause, stop, and check in with myself and do the right thing.

10. TRANSFORMATION

Slow down.
Pause for a moment.
Let in, the springtime unfolding.
Let in, the gleam in a child's eyes.
Let in, the water that is coming down.
Let in, the passion.
Let in, the wonder.
Let in, the tenderness of your heart.
Let in the light.
Surrender.
Come back to your source right here, right now.

— ÖÖ

In high school I was convinced that I was ugly and definitely not an interesting person and no man would ever fall in love with me. When finishing high school and starting university men started showing interest in me. Initially, I wasn't sure if this was real since I still believed that I wasn't interesting enough, then after spending more time with men I became convinced they were definitely interested in me, especially in my physical appearance. Slowly, my ugly perception about myself switched to partly believing that I was beautiful at seventeen years old. While I thought during my university years that guys liked my looks and had a particular crush on my long wavy hair, I never believed that they also liked my personality or that they liked who I was. Did they like my flaws, my anger, or my shyness? What about my confidence, my drive, my knowledge, how I talked, did they like my body with all its imperfections? Where did my failures and insecurities stand? I wasn't sure if I liked all these parts about myself, so how could any man like these as well? I didn't believe a guy would love me with all of these attributes, so I chose for most of the time to be distant to a guy. Yet in the end, I was also a human being, at times very sensitive and with strong feelings.

One of the times I felt butterflies in my tummy was when I started liking a guy at university. After he told me I was beautiful, intelligent and very kind, I immediately fell for him because he had said the very things I craved to hear. Being convinced that I was not that intelligent and wasn't kind at all, I tried very hard to be more intelligent and kind but it was never enough for me. After a few months I decided to break up with this guy even though the relationship hadn't really progressed. I was scared to be rejected if he got to know me better and see my other attributes. I was incredibly shy with men, hesitant of physical touch, and fearful to show who I really was. The only thing I wanted to show was the pretense of being this confident girl in all areas of her life but she was too proud to not be vulnerable and show her unconfident human side. Shortly after not seeing this guy anymore, I fell into a few platonic loves. During these platonic loves, I loved going to bed early, putting my comforter on my head and dreaming about my platonic love. I was dreaming about how much I loved him and how much he loved me and how entangled our souls could be with each other. The years went by and I kept having the same patterns of being desperately, platonically in love with someone. Sometimes I took a small step towards that person, but when the guy became a bit closer to me and started looking into my soul, I felt intimidated and became immediately distant. I never wanted to commit.

When the time was right there came a moment when I decided to get over my fear and the Universe reacted to this. I met a guy I started showing parts of my soul. Slowly I showed parts of who I was to him because I started to slowly believe that he loved who I was, regardless of my insecurities. I had never done this before, so I didn't know how it worked. I felt that I just had to try. Opening my soul to him meant freely loving him. There were so many years that I was very hesitant to show any man my emotions or thoughts freely. I was kind of compensating and giving all the love to this guy at the moment. Before I was aware, I was slowly starting to lose myself to the idea of being in love with him. Today, I would call it madness and obsession. I started losing sight of other things and couldn't see what he was also not. I only wanted to see his perfection. I was partly in love with him, but a bigger part was that I was lost in him, lost in the idea of being in love with him. I couldn't see that we had different visions in life and instead of enriching each other, after a while we started limiting each other. While I felt I was fully committed to this relationship, I could sense that he wasn't. Even though I could feel that he wasn't committed, I didn't want to admit it because I only wanted to see the good parts of being with him and on top of that I believed he was filling my gaps and insecurities. After being on and off several times and being tired of it, we decided to break up permanently. It was a bitter decision because at the time I believed that we loved each other. But there were two sides of the coin. When we started being together, I believed that he loved me because of my personality, but on the other hand, I wasn't sure if my personality and background fit into his image for the girlfriend he wanted to have. As devastated I was, he was the first guy I had revealed my true self to which I had been hesitant to do for years and at the end, I felt rejected by the person because of who I was. With being more angry at myself Rumi's words came to my mind then: *"Are you offended by the hand that does not hold your hand or are you*

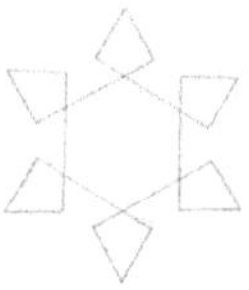

I was at the end of my twenties and angry at myself that I had held out my hand to someone who hadn't wanted to hold it. So I looked back at my life. What was my whole life about? As a teenager I thought I had to figure "it" all out by reaching the age of thirty; being married with the love of my life, owning property, having plenty of cash in my bank account, and having at least one child. And here I was, I just came out of a relationship, moved back to Amsterdam from living in Istanbul, didn't own any property or have plenty of cash, and I didn't have children. While crying myself to sleep became a habitual night routine, the pain of the break-up swallowed me each day a little bit more with the expanding story I created in my mind. I felt like a victim and I started taking refuge in writing, calligraphy, nature and started turning my attention to nature and people that provided me with unconditional love. While grief, sadness and anger alternated for a period of time in my whole being, I eventually came to a point where I realized that falling in love and even maybe feeling lost in someone was a necessary experience in order to connect to my true power and transform myself.

Yearning to find fulfillment, I met Jacob. Being from the other side of the world, a place in the Pacific Ocean, he lived with his wife and son in Amsterdam. First, I believed that Jacob had figured "it" all out: he had come from far lands and built a family and career. I wanted to be just as successful as he was. Success for me was measured in terms of building a family, career, professional and material achievements. Thinking that I wanted to be as successful as Jacob was, I realized that I was tying my worth and joy in life to things outside of myself. Paradoxical as it was, Jacob valued success in different terms than I did; in terms of compassion, understanding, tolerance, kindness and service to others. He was one of the few people who treated me with unconditional compassion, gave unconditional love, and believed in me as a person which I hadn't encountered for a long time. The support of only one compassionate person was the start of my journey of self-reflection.

During the conversations we had I started revealing to him my true self and parts of my soul. By doing honest self examination I learned to fully accept not only my light but also my darkness. Unexpectedly as it was, the more authentic I started to be, the more Jacob's unconditional compassion expanded. Actually, I never heard Jacob say he loved me, but he gave me love. He was the brother that you want to have who is genuinely appreciating you and is on your side, regardless of whatever it is you're facing. He made me believe in my own wings to fly. Jacob was the friend you want to have who accepts you as you are and respects all your imperfections that you might even refuse to accept in yourself. His being exposed me to the truths in myself and when I opened to these truths, my vulnerability became my true power. Angels come in many forms and Jacob was one of them. In my loneliness and grief, seeking love, his wisdom and love helped me go on. He kept sending me love and light and accepted me just as I was. I could tell him anything and all he did was listen and appreciate. First, thinking that he agreed with all what I thought, I realized that he didn't always agree with me but he appreciated who I was and what I was feeling. As powerful as it was, with his appreciation I started being more open and aware to parts of myself that I kept trying to fight for years. I started recognizing my soul and the parts of my being in life. Slowly, my worth and joy in life that I had tied to things outside of myself started to move to things inside of me. Also, in those times of grief I visited Alyssa Monks' words who said:

> 'We're all going to have big losses in our lives, maybe a job or a career, relationships, love, our youth. We're going to lose our health, people we love. These kinds of losses are out of our control. They're unpredictable, and they bring us to our knees. And so I say, let them. Fall to your knees. Be humbled. Let go of trying to change it or even wanting it to be different. It just is. And then there's space, and in that space feel your vulnerability, what matters most to you, your deepest intention. And be curious to connect to what and who is really here, awake and alive. It's what we all want. Let's take the opportunity to find something beautiful in the unknown, in the unpredictable, and even in the awful.'

It was time I chose to walk a different path. I started embracing my inner child. Jacob, selflessly, was holding a space for me to express the deepest truth of who I was. Instead of putting out what happens outside of myself, I started looking inside. I always thought that I was this ugly fearless girl who just did it, yet I realized the real courage came from being vulnerable, looking inside myself and loving myself just as I am. I started to embrace my perfections and imperfections. Bit-by-bit, I became comfortable with my flaws, learned to appreciate my drive, accept my sadness and anger, like the way I look, and most importantly, to love myself. It was not always easy, but I started embracing the difficulties and became more comfortable with the uncomfortable. After shedding some light on myself, connecting to my source, and believing in my own power that was fueled by love and compassion, I started transforming my being into a more authentic version of myself.

11. HIGHER POWER

When you walk, only walk in goodness.
When you talk, sweeten your tongue, sweeter than honey.
When you look, look as if seeing the eyes of your lover.
When you listen, be in the story of the teller.

— ÖÖ

Since I was four years old, my parents sent me every weekend to the Turkish mosque close by home. I truly loved and still love going to the mosque. Many children, mostly girls, went to this mosque. Waking up on a Saturday morning with a cup of tea and biscuits, I'd hurry through breakfast, collect the girls in the neighborhood and run to the mosque, literally run, because I couldn't wait to learn. If this was a church or a Japanese course instead of a mosque, I'd go. Learning new things was my thing. Wherever I could learn there was life for me.

My parents had chosen this mosque and I started evolving my learning ability there. The mosque that I went to was known by most people from Alkmaar, but from the outside it didn't look like a classic mosque as I used to see during the summer holidays in almost every village and neighborhood in Turkey. The mosque in Alkmaar was in fact an old Dutch school building, without minarets. While the architecture of the building wasn't similar to a typical mosque in Turkey, the interior architecture and design were slightly transformed the way a mosque might look. While the area for women was divided from the area for men, the building was equipped with loudspeakers to make sure all could hear the sermons of the imam and common prayers. The carpet flooring was covered with prayer rugs, characterized by a niche at one end, facing the mihrap on the mosque wall made of blue tiles. They made sure that the prayer rug and the mihrap were both facing the direction of Mecca. The placement of the mihrap, the pulpit where the imam delivers Friday sermons, was positioned to the right of the mihrap, and with all of these it became a real mosque in my eyes.

As my learning ability kept expanding, the mosque became a continuous learning space. I experienced learning as something fun and easy. I learned fast, but at the moment I saw others learning faster than me and I got stuck in stress and then learned even slower. I was stressed because what if the other person performed better than me? I would feel bad and less than others. I didn't want to feel less. I wanted to feel good and one direct way to this feeling was competing until I felt the best. Competitiveness was somehow in my whole being. At the mosque, I first learned Arabic letters and then read the Quran in Arabic. My first Quran was a small red one, which

I still have today. Each spring I got some flowers and put them between the pages in my Quran to dry and it gave the Quran a great smell. Since I was a fast learner, I knew in a couple of weeks how to read the Quran. As crazy as it sounds, I actually never knew the meaning of the text that I was reading, unless the imam explained it to me from time-to-time. It wasn't taught by default and since I didn't have an easy access to the Quran in any other language than Arabic, I wasn't intrinsically motivated to reread the Arabic verses in Turkish or Dutch. As weird as it still is to me, I was never exposed to learning the meaning of the Quran. The curriculum of the Quran education that was sent to the mosque in the Netherlands by the Turkish government didn't provide the subject of learning the meaning. I still wonder why that was. Was it because it was better to not bother students with the meaning so they wouldn't question anything and just take what they heard for granted? Was it that they didn't want to bother people with extra homework? Or was it because this was an easy way to control people?

Besides reciting the Quran, I learned about Islam in general, the five pillars of Islam, and the Islamic schools and branches. It was very peaceful being in the mosque, but there were moments that I felt restless and scared: the time when the imam taught us what wasn't allowed in Islam and what could happen to you if you did the things that were considered "forbidden." As a child, I had difficulty with things that were restricted and the punishments that belonged to it. I found it difficult to understand that God would punish people and I actually didn't want to believe that because I was so scared. How could a source that created me also punish me? How could God punish people whereas he has in Islam ninety-nine divine attributes, *Asma'ul-Husna* (أسماء الله الحسنى), such as being the most gracious, the most merciful, the most sacred, ever forgiving and the nourisher? A much more peaceful concept that I learned in the mosque was, *"As an individual, it isn't on you to judge another human being on being a good or bad person, the beingness of that person is unique for himself and it has a secret way of being."* I had decided that moment to take this sentence with me for my whole life; I believed if God created all, there must be a reason that we are all different and unique. I definitely have days that I know this sentence and don't live by it, but this sentence helps me appreciate the other person only because of his or her "being" and nothing more or less.

Years went by, I kept going to the mosque on weekends for a long time and after I turned seventeen I stopped going to focus on my studies at the University. I also knew that there was more out there than the mosque in Alkmaar that I visited. I became more interested in philosophy and wanted to learn about other religions, especially Eastern religions. In this exploration phase, I started reading about philosophy, other religions, consciousness, and writings from Persian and Lebanese poets and writings from Rumi. While I was a bit confused if I was cheating on the religion that I thought I had to hold onto or always have with me, each book gave me insights about what is important in life and made me more aware of myself. While each writing was focused on compassion, love and goodness, I constantly reconnected the writings I read with the sentence said by the imam of the mosque from my childhood, "*As an individual, it isn't on you to judge another human being on being a good or bad person, the beingness of that person is unique for himself and it has a secret way of being.*" I recognized my belief in the mystery of each individual being which is connected to everyone. I decided that I could see what I wanted to see in each individual, the good, the bad, or both. I realized I am in control to decide whether I love and see the love in the other being. In order to see good and love, first I have to be good and love myself.

2016 - Florida, United States

As nice as the words sound, theory and practice were something from completely different dimensions. On one hand, you can know that goodness and love is in all of us and sometimes we only need a light to help recognize it in ourselves. On the other hand, you can experience goodness and love in practice. For me, true light was offered through living examples of goodness and love through daily situations, sometimes at random places and in numerous cultures and countries by different people, regardless of their belief system.

When attending an awareness course in Florida, I met a trainer. Initially, because of my own projection this trainer appeared to me as someone who was not a friendly person. I was a bit afraid of her, scared that she would be direct and tough on me and hurt my feelings. During the course, I went to her with a question very important to me. It was a long question. I wanted to make sure that I explained this question well so I stood there and started explaining at great length. Although I was hesitant, I kept going. While I was thinking that she would think I am stupid and that I didn't know much and perhaps think I was unable to figure things out for myself, I later realized I was actually judging myself and not her at all. To my surprise, the trainer only listened with appreciation. While asking the question, she was there with me in my thoughts, muddling through this question. While I was nervous of her reaction, she was there with my nervousness. While judging myself on the long question I had to ask, she was there with me. She was fully present. This trainer was truly strong and most importantly, she was authentic. She found a place in herself to lift me up by appreciating me. She didn't teach me appreciation with any theory, she taught me by doing it and making me feel how it is to be appreciated.

Experiencing theory and practice as different dimensions, I found a way to connect the two: theory touches the mind and the practice of the theory connects to the heart. When moving from mind to heart I was able to receive goodness and see the goodness in others. When being still, truly listening and appreciating others and enjoying the beingness of that person, which is unique and has a secret way of being, something cracks in our hearts. Appreciation is the magic of opening the heart to another heart.

12. TRUST

The tree in front of our door.
Tells us more than it just is.
It tells us our nature.
It tells us our being.
Let the root of the tree remind us of our heart.
Which gives life to our branches and makes us blossom.
And when the time is right, we let go of our leaves.
And grow new ones.

— ÖÖ

I grew up in a small public housing apartment not more than sixty square meters. Our living room was very small and the three bedrooms were even smaller. Every single bedroom was fitted with exactly one bed—my parents had a double bed, my brother a twin bed, and my sister and I slept in a bunk bed in a nine square meter room. In the whole apartment, we had one gas heater, which was placed in the living room. During the winter months my parents turned the heater on only during evening until midnight to the highest degree and we opened all the bedroom doors in the house so the heat could be felt throughout, making sure there was enough warmth before we slept. The nicest part of this gas heater was putting a pillow in front of it and laying down next to it with the television on in front of me. My mother used this gas heater to also heat the pot of Turkish tea which she served us every evening. Because our bedrooms were not that warm during cold winter days, the living room became my private room where I did homework, watched television, drew, and read. In my shared bedroom with my sister, there was enough space for a two-door wardrobe and a small desk where I could do my homework. In our bedroom, we had a door opening to the balcony with a view of the highway and surrounding greenery or the clothes that my mother hung on the balcony.

As a child I liked from time-to-time to be by myself, read and draw. I loved drawing people and creating a poem next to the drawings. I wasn't sure if it was my oversensitivity, but I didn't like lots of sounds around me. Something in me got extremely distracted and anxious when I heard many sounds mixed up, especially when I had to focus on something. As much fun as it was and as safe as I felt to sleep with my sister in our bedroom, I was usually distracted by sounds. For instance, when I did homework she might walk behind me or someone next door might take a shower and the noise and movement would disturb my focus. Yet, I was very ambivalent about being alone in the bedroom. When I found myself alone in the bedroom, the stillness could be very peaceful, yet also lonely.

My favorite room in this apartment was my brother's room, which we had previously shared together before my sister was born.

It was spacious and bright. When my brother wasn't in it I liked to hang out in that room. The reason I loved this room so much was because of the trees outside. There was a big tree exactly in front of the window. At the root of this tree were little holes where I used to play marble with other children, especially boys, in the neighborhood. I used to watch the tree, almost every day, watching and waiting for the change to begin, to catch the tree in the moment of changing. Even though I loved and still love summer as my favorite season, I admired the transformation of the tree during the change of season from summer to autumn. The leaves turned into shades of yellow, brown and orange. And then, one by one, they fell or flew away. Every single day the tree let more and more leaves go until it was all bare. It was empty, bold, at the same time strong. I loved gazing at the tree on cold winter days when it was so cold that the inside of the windows became moist. When it was a light blue sky and the sun was shining the tree stood there, when it was foggy and pouring rain the tree stood there. For a few months the tree didn't change, it only "was." I could dream and feel the tree. It became my daily friend which I could greet. While I was verbally communicating with everyone in the house, my communication with the tree was only based on feeling each other. The tree started slowly changing, like I and my whole family did. As Heraclitus observed, everything was constantly shifting, changing and becoming something else from what it was before. The tree changed slowly, day-by-day, one-by-one, buds on the branches. I always wondered how this tree survived the whole winter. The buds came back, one-by-one, and then slowly I saw a very small green leaf. And then another and another and one more. The tree "was," and it got leaves. The more sun and spring rain there was, the more leaves there were that grew from the tree. Now it wasn't easy to see the view behind the tree. It was also difficult for my mother to wave to us until we turned the corner of the street because the tree blocked the view with all of its leaves. And then, in the summer the tree was full of green leaves.

However, after leaving this apartment and living by myself, I forgot to look at trees for a while. Nowadays, I still look at trees, especially when I am too much in my head, thinking of what the future will bring or what the past has to say. When I look at a tree, I can feel that the tree "just is" and that "I just am." There is no need to think, there is only observation without judgement. There is only beauty and respect to a tree, which stands and only "is." It was there when it slowly lost its leaves in the rain and wind. It was also there in cold winter days when it was empty. The spring sun and rain gave the tree new leaves and it transformed. In summer time, the tree was ready for many leaves.

Having started with the tree exactly in front of the window of my brother's room, trees remind me of an importance in my own life: being present. Like a tree, give up looking and just "be," regardless of the circumstances. Have trust in your own nature and journey. Like the tree, everything and everyone will arrive at the right time and depart at the right time. Just "be" and embrace you.

13. PEACE

Pause for a moment.
Let your mind and body melt at the same place at the same time.
There is a purposefulness of slowing down.
Move half as fast, notice twice as much.
There is no time to rush.

— ÖÖ

Istanbul, formerly Constantinople, the transcontinental city in Turkey, could be like a drug for me. While I have never used chemical drugs, I kept saying Istanbul was like a drug to me. At some moments the city drove me crazy and I wanted to leave immediately but at the same time, I loved it as I didn't love any city before. It's something I loved and still love so much because it also kept me sane and alive. Istanbul was and still is like a spark that I don't feel anywhere else in the world. Something without words, without form.

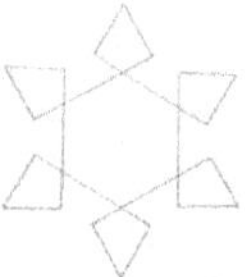

On a typical Sunday when I left my home in the neighborhood of Nişantaşı, the only thing I wanted to do was to take refuge from the busyness of the city: the voices of the people in the textile street where I was living, the lights that were never turned off in Nişantaşı, people constantly moving to get somewhere, the honking yellow taxis and street vendors trying to sell water and simit—the circular bread with sesame seeds. Working with small children at the international school was satisfying and at the same time tiring. Living on the sixth floor at the top of the apartment building in a narrow street didn't make it easier to take refuge either. The buildings were close to each other, a textile business operated in the heart of Nişantaşı, fancy cars that were either really old or brand new were constantly thrumming the narrow streets, shopping malls and busy people all filled the view and created a ruckus of sounds all around me.

I sometimes felt that I couldn't control the busyness, my mind was spinning from all the noise and pace around me. Yet it was something I resisted and desired at the same time. Istanbul had a flare, which I didn't feel anywhere else. People lived either a Western life, a more traditional life, or a mix of both. Living in the blend of these three lifestyles was what I loved the most. Even though I sometimes thought my Western clothing made me look very

Western, from the inside I knew that I was a very traditional and sometimes old-fashioned person. However, when I lived in Istanbul I found it difficult to admit my traditional and old-fashioned side to myself and to others. Struggling for years with it, I eventually came to a point that I accept and love it. I started defining traditional for me as feeling the core of the seed that was one day planted. When taking it one step further, I could feel the core of the seed that has created me and the core of the creator of that seed and so on. Simply, my family has been living in a Western world, the Netherlands, only since 1968. That meant to be born in this Western world, it gave me many privileges which I am grateful for and never could have imagined otherwise. On the other hand, feeling the core of all seeds that are connected to me makes me connect to Turkey and without exactly knowing where my ancestors are from I mysteriously have a deep connection to Anatolia, Turkey. Whenever I am on the ground in Anatolia, I feel that I am home but I feel at the same time that I am a foreigner. It's a feeling that anyone who has been an immigrant could understand.

By leaving my home in Nişantaşı my instinct told me to go to the old city, Sultan Ahmet. Sultan Ahmet meant for me the area to connect with not only the history of Istanbul, but the history of the world as far as I can grasp in my consciousness. Being in the presence of two holy buildings in this old city, the Hagia Sophia and Sultan Ahmet Mosque, was sacred to me. The Hagia Sophia was built during the Byzantine empire in 537 and Sultan Ahmet was built by the Ottoman Empire in 1616. While both buildings were initially built for religious purposes, Hagia Sophia as a church and Sultan Ahmet as mosque, the two buildings in the heart of Istanbul could receive and connect people from all over the world. While both buildings with its domes and minarets stood the test of time and were still standing, when entering those buildings I could feel the immediate change in most people. Something invisible and ungraspable was happening. It was as if the hearts of people were expanding and in a moment of time they were experiencing and shining with peace and compassion. I call it moving from head to heart. These historical and at the same time spiritual buildings' ceilings reached up to heaven, inviting humans to connect with a higher source. As the meaning of Hagia Sophia is "holy wisdom," each time when I am in the presence of this area with the two spiritual places I feel peace. I never get tired of visiting this area and each time I visit it again the holy presence touches my soul in new ways. A deep sense of gratitude arises when I am there.

Killing time observing people in the buzzed metro from Osmanbey to the metro stop Şişhane, a tram awaited to take us passengers over the Galata bridge towards the old city. The Haliç, the water under the Galata bridge, was its best blue ever. The pigeons were flying close to all the ferries that were on the Haliç to get pieces of simit from ferry passengers. On the left I could feel the presence of the Hagia Sophia, its massive dome making it a landmark to all nearby. Another gem, the Sultan Ahmet mosque, constructed ten centuries after the Hagia Sophia, shone brightly under the light of the sun. Just the view of these two buildings gave me peace and I could feel the source of my being. History was looking at me and I was looking at history.

Somehow by mistake I got out a few stops earlier and I found myself just behind the Grand Bazaar. The sounds on the street became louder, men were selling spices, Turkish delights, olives, dried eggplants, dry fruit, cheese and more of the food I knew from my childhood summer visits to Turkey. Trying to navigate myself to the road towards Hagia Sophia and Sultan Ahmet Mosque I realized that I was in a sort of maze and standing in front of an open grey door, framed by large smooth stones expertly fitted into an arch. I passed through the doorway, and began to slowly climb the stone steps up a dark staircase until I emerged into a breathtaking courtyard. I had to pause, take in the view of the architecture, the wall decorated by the Iznik and Kütahya blue tiles of the Ottoman Tile Art and I heard someone whispering the name of the mosque I was at: "Rüstem Paşa Mosque."

Everything was quiet, time stood still, no sounds came from the buzzing Grand Bazaar, even the birds were resting on the edge of the fence of Rüstem Paşa. I didn't know you could get more silence than silence itself, it was so serene. The gentleman at the entrance with a prayer cap on his head welcomed me with a candid smile. And so here I was, in Rüstem Paşa, with a few other locals, just breathing. Although *namaz*, the Muslim Prayer, had not been a part of my daily practice, in Rüstem Paşa I strongly felt the desire to participate in *namaz*. I fell to my knees and my head touched the floor. Afterwards, I just sat. Tears of gratitude trickled down my face. The whole world started and stopped here, I just "was." I surrendered to "being."

IN CONCLUSION

One of the most important things that I have learned in life is **"I decide."** Whether it is believing in yourself or doubting yourself, judging someone or seeing goodness in someone, you decide what your reality is! You are responsible for your own life and change what you want to see in the world. Every thought in your mind and every word you speak is powerful, so choose them deliberately.

There isn't a perfect world, it's up to you to make it perfect. It's up to you to take it all in, stop taking things for granted, and start appreciating life and human beings. If everything would be perfect we wouldn't have the chance to appreciate our world. Be grateful and recognize the little things in life that make you happy instead of complaining about what you don't have.

Lead your life with your heart. Don't forget that you are human with all your imperfections. Spread yourself around the universe in a way that is authentically you and never stop being yourself. Wherever you can find yourself, follow it: at your spiritual place, at home, in your classroom, at work, with your friends. Lean on that strength of your inner self.

Stop leading yourself by **fear**, stop **distrusting** others and throw out your **biases** and **judgement**s about others and yourself. Find in every **resistance** a chance to get to know yourself. Lead with **kindness** and **authenticity**. Rip your **past & future** thoughts into a thousand pieces and don't leave any room for **pride & ego.** Believe in that **higher power**, whatever that is for you and **trust** that all imperfections of the universe will lead you exactly at the right time to the right **transformation.** And most importantly, wherever you can be in **peace**, be it!

ACKNOWLEDGEMENTS

While I am grateful to many people who were an inspiration for me to write this book and have been my life teachers, I want to show my gratitude to some people who have made a significant contribution to make this book happen.

Writing this book started with an idea which developed further with many trial and errors which lead to the creation of this actual book. First of all, I want to show my gratitude and appreciation to my friend Mariah for being with me all the way through writing this book, also during the trial and errors and beyond. While working full time, having a newborn and a time difference of six hours, she worked day and night with me to edit my writing, coach me, and most importantly give me selfless support and unconditional love. Without Mariah this book wouldn't be here as it is now.

I would like to express my love and gratitude to my extended family Aynur, Jay and Kadriye. Thanks for teaching me to be bold and look inside of myself and make me believe in myself. Without your unconditional compassion, appreciation and love, I wouldn't have started writing this book. Thanks for your unlimited patience with me and always being there.

I am thankful for my friends who live in different parts of the world. You know who you are. I am grateful that our paths have crossed and each of you have taught me something that is now a part of me. I feel honored and grateful that you are part of my life. You have been wonderful to me.

Thank you to my students who I was privileged to teach. Thanks for showing me how easy it is to show your true self and just "be." And as we had placed on our classroom board "my happiest moments in life," one of my happiest moments was with you.

I am grateful to everyone who I have worked with. Without your trust in me, I wouldn't have those experiences and have the fuel of writing this book.

And my parents, who gave me life and my siblings who shared life with me, thank you for your unconditional love and always wanting the best for me. You made me experience life and made me the person I am now.

ABOUT THE AUTHOR

Özlem Özkan is a culturally diverse woman, based in Amsterdam, the Netherlands. Born and raised in the Netherlands, she has also lived in Istanbul, Turkey and Aarhus, Denmark; and traveled across continents. Due to her bicultural identity she constantly moved between East and West but also in her heart and mind. Özlem is grateful for all the formal education she has achieved (Bachelor degree in Education, Master degree in Educational Sciences), for this has provided her with ways of thinking, allowed her to gain knowledge, and developed her intellect. Wisdom is what she gathered during her travels, work, living abroad, spending time alone, and interacting with various people from different layers of society.

She isn't fearless! She also has fears, yet she moves forward comfortably uncomfortable!

Follow Özlem on Instagram and Facebook for continuous updates via @ozkanozlem and www.ozkanozlem.com.

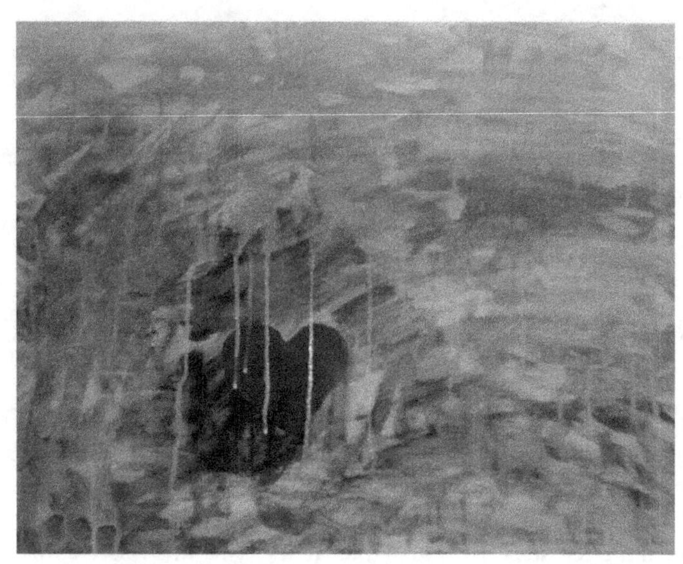

Painting by author "My heart remains in chaos".